$\mathcal{H}$ealing Through Psalm 23
Life—Journey with the Unknown

Inseong J. Kim
&
Elizabeth Fair

WESTBOW
PRESS®
A DIVISION OF THOMAS NELSON
& ZONDERVAN

This book is a work of non-fiction. Unless otherwise noted, the author and the publisher
make no explicit guarantees as to the accuracy of the information contained in this book
and in some cases, names of people and places have been altered to protect their privacy.

WestBow Press books may be ordered through booksellers or by contacting:

WestBow Press
A Division of Thomas Nelson & Zondervan
1663 Liberty Drive
Bloomington, IN 47403
www.westbowpress.com
1 (866) 928-1240

Because of the dynamic nature of the Internet, any web addresses or links contained in
this book may have changed since publication and may no longer be valid. The views
expressed in this work are solely those of the author and do not necessarily reflect the
views of the publisher, and the publisher hereby disclaims any responsibility for them.

Any people depicted in stock imagery provided by Getty Images are
models, and such images are being used for illustrative purposes only.
Certain stock imagery © Getty Images.

Cover image credit: Inseong J. Kim
www.inseonggallery.com

ISBN: 978-1-9736-5775-0 (sc)
ISBN: 978-1-9736-5776-7 (hc)
ISBN: 978-1-9736-5774-3 (e)

Library of Congress Control Number: 2019903389

Print information available on the last page.

WestBow Press rev. date: 3/27/2019

ഇൻ ൻ

Dedicated to the precious sheep who are trusting God as
you seek to grow and mature in wisdom, knowledge and
your relationship with God. He is faithful to transform you
with His unfailing Word, full of Love, Grace and Truth.
Soli Deo Gloria!

Contents

Acknowledgements

The Light of Christianity can only be transferred by
showing God's grace in a real way. -Inseong J. Kim

Forgiveness is something that we often take lightly with pride by judging others who we cannot forgive until we ourselves go through the valley of shadow of death by others who have wronged us, especially when we are young and vulnerable. As we get older, we question our lives, our worldview and ultimately God who allowed all those painful moments of our lives to happen.

We often remain distant from God, trying to figure things out, but as we go through our life journey, we later find out that God loves us enough to take on everything! He died. He took all the responsibility, gave us the shield of His Righteousness and was then Raised back to life and invites us to share in His abundant Life!

I want to thank those who share the love of Christ with the labor of prayer and love.

Phoenix Seminary, for training leaders diligently as Scholars with Shepherd's heart.

Dr. Darryl DelHousaye, a scholar with a shepherd's heart & Mrs. Holly DelHousaye, a quiet, yet strong mentor and prayer warrior.

The word ringing in my ears from the pastor Darryl DelHousaye, *"Inseong, you are living in the land of mercy."* He was right. How many times I experienced God's favor in my life! Despite my painful memory, my journey of healing blooms when I am counting His Blessings, His Goodness, His Mercy and His Grace. My encouragement for those who are suffering from this broken world is to study with me through this journey of exploring the deep treasures within Psalm 23.

I thank everyone who serves at Phoenix Seminary, who are there for the wounded and broken. Phoenix Seminary is not just an educational institution for scholars, but also shepherds with the heart of God where we can learn hands on ministry, how we ought to serve the wounded, one on one, by battling with each soul carefully and sincerely listening.

I thank God for the great teaching from Calvary Community Church at Phoenix Arizona about God's grace.

David and JoAnne Everett who founded Crisis Pregnancy Center in Phoenix, their labor of love for many unborn babies and parents.

Elizabeth Fair who co-authored Psalm 23 with the labor of love and one heart.

1360AM KPXQ Salem Communication and Wilkins Communication, their deep understanding the nature of our ministry and support. General Manager, Jim Ryan, Program Director Tom Brown's testimony and Jeremy Segal who records our program each week with enthusiasm and encouragement!

I want to sincerely thank those who faithfully listen to my story and prayed for me to be healed so that I can say "It is well with my soul."

Thank you for everyone who journeyed with me whether a small way or big way! There are no words for me to say how thankful I am.

Sincerely,

Inseong J. Kim

"Give a man a fish, feed him for a day. Teach a man to fish, feed him for a lifetime" – Ancient Proverb

Greetings in the Name of Our Lord Jesus Christ, God's Grace & Peace be with You!

Thank you to my Heavenly Father, Almighty God, Creator of the Universe who loves me, chose me and is beautifully at work redeeming this broken world.

Thank you to my beloved friends and family (especially Mom & Sarah Knutson). For your love, support, prayers, encouragement, patience, perseverance and life experiences that God then culminated to bring this book about.

Thank you to you who are reading this, may God be Awesomely Glorified through this book with Great Victory in and through your Life.

God, You Rock!

With much Love in Christ,

Elizabeth Fair

Introduction

From the first step of a baby to the grave, we hold the Heavenly Father's hand and venture our life together with good and bad......and at the end, we cherish everything with thanksgiving. – Inseong J. Kim

From the time we are born, we are so full of imagination with wonder and awe. Some are born in a warm and cozy nest, others are born with unanswered quests. We all search for happiness and run toward our dreams and hope in believing we all can get there. We do not know why we are born nor how we got here, but the warm and gentle hands guide us through and through in His grace...

Families and friends with laughter blossom the journey of adventure. We all wish the best in our lives without any sadness or tears. As summer comes, our unknown journey is tainted with heartbeat wonder, which comes sometimes through the storm even as a hurricane, sometimes as a gentle breeze with the faint scent of spring. As we believe we will arrive at the place where all is well, we can still have hope for today. The season tells us time to go on, we arise to finish well just as the wildflowers give all their strength to bless us with the gift of grace. *Yesterday Today Tomorrow Program*

When I was driving to the radio station, there were orange poppy flowers blooming along the I-10 in Arizona. It is unusual for flowers to bloom in the midst of the blistering hot weather of Arizona in August. I think the poppies were confused thinking it was spring! We had been experiencing such amazing weather and even some rain. Studying Psalm 23 was a precious moment in this season of my life. I hope this book can be a blessing to those who are in the season of searching, like the beautiful refreshing poppies in the midst of difficult weather.

God gave me a passion to comfort those who have gone through similar pain like I did. I found the astronomical numbers of people on this planet, who went through abortion, yet could not even verbalize it because of the severe pain. Many do not even know what happen to them. I am blessed to have a platform to share my story. Through sharing my story, I was able to be released from the unspoken pain, anger and my grief. By comforting others, God comforted me. My sincere appreciation is due to many of those who prayed for us.

Through this humble book, may God comfort you who are suffering from the unexpected tragedy in your life or loss of a loved one, yet who still needs to forgive and understand the province of God in an eternal perspective. May God grant you with the wisdom and knowledge to understand the Word of God in a different level with His deep insight. May God open your eyes to see the unseen world and be a prayer warrior for God's Kingdom.

The purpose of this book, Psalm 23, *Life Journey of Unknown*, is to comfort and commission both shepherds and sheep in the churches as well as lost sheep everywhere as our Good Shepherd continues to draw us into His sheepfold. Through the study of Psalm 23, I pray we walk deeper with God and safely rest in the place of contentment where we can say with confidence, "It is well with my soul."

I have written to you who are God's children because you know the Father. I have written to you who are mature in the faith because you know Christ, who existed from the beginning. I have written to you who are young in the faith because you are strong. God's word lives in your hearts, and you have won your battle with the evil one. (1 John 2:14 NLT)

Background
Please Read Psalm 22-24

$\mathcal{T}$he book of Psalms is written by various authors to express their joys and sorrows, frustration and praise, and supplication and truth. Any of us can relate to the messages and songs delivered in the Psalms.

Many of the Psalms were written by King David, son of Jesse, a man who started out as a young shepherd boy, who tended to his sheep and was known for playing the harp and making a new song for the Lord. This young shepherd boy grew up to become a mighty warrior who became a beloved King over Israel and was called a "man after God's own heart." Psalm 23 is a particularly simple, yet powerful psalm written by David.

Psalm 23 is one of the most quoted sections of scripture. Even soldiers at war have been known to recite this Psalm when they are distressed at war to experience the peace that only comes from God. When we recognize the spiritual portion of our lives, we can find Psalm 23 to be of great comfort to overcome fear, distress, and anguish with an incredible hope.

A major key word of Psalm 23 is shepherd. The author, King David described God as Shepherd. There are 15 main verbs: is (to be), not want, make lie down, lead, restores, guide, walk, fear, are with, comfort, prepare, anoint, overflows, follow, dwell. These verbs show us how God loves and takes care of us and the opportunity we have to respond to this special relationship we can have with God.

Psalm 23 is formed with only 6 verses, but it is easily broken down into ten subjects to study together for twelve weeks (with the background and conclusion). We could study Psalm 23 for a lifetime and still find deeper applications because God's word is living and active, exposing our innermost thoughts and desires and God is continually at work in your life, drawing you closer to Himself, if we choose to listen and follow. I can only reveal a glimpse of Psalm 23 so that the Holy Spirit has a foundation to reveal God's Hope, Healing and Truth through the treasures in Psalm 23. He delights to show you those treasures in Psalm 23.

To place Psalm 23 into context, it is helpful to review Psalm 22 and Psalm 24 because these are the words that precede and follow Psalm 23, allowing us to better unpack and understand the richness of the treasures found within the six verses of Psalm 23.

An overview of Psalm 22 opens the passage with the same words that Jesus quotes while on the cross as recorded in Matthew 27:46 and Mark 15:34.

> *My God, my God, why have you forsaken me? Why are you so far from saving me, from the words of my groaning? O my God, I cry by day, but you do not answer, and by night, but I find no rest. (Psalm 22:1-2)*

These verses are also cited at the site of crucifixion in Matthew 27:46; Mark 15:34.

Jesus was quoting Psalm 22 when He was crucified, not only because He was experiencing the great pain and sorrow of humanity but also because He was revealing to the people that He is the Messiah whom they yearn and have been waiting to see. Psalm 22 continues on with David's struggles with his internal and external enemies, the knowledge of trusting God as his Savior and the attitude of his heart. The passage also recognizing the praise, beauty and sovereignty of the Lord who rules over the earth and nations.

Psalm 24 follows Psalm 23, declaring the King of Glory entering Israel. We can watch the progression of the attitude of David's heart from Psalm 22 to Psalm 24 and can see the divine attributes of God and His Glory. We can see the relation between our status in the Psalm 24:4 with "clean hands and the pure heart" and the entrance of God's Kingdom and the victory that belongs to the King of Kings and Lord of Lords.

When we understand the reality that God is the King of Glory who loves us and desires to make all things new and allow Him to transform the attitude of our hearts, then we can begin on the path of living a holy life, which is our spiritual act of worship to this Great and Glorious God.

Psalm 22 presents the conditions for glory displayed in Psalm 24. When we have clean hands and pure hearts through Christ, and then God's Glory will enter in through His grace. God commissions us to live the life of holiness, as the redeemed children of God who were bought by the blood of Jesus.

By clear understanding our Identity in Christ, we can have the healthy view of the world through that lens or filter. Let us begin our adventure with God by reading Psalm 23.

Psalm 23 – The Lord is My Shepherd

The Lord is my Shepherd;
I shall not want.
He makes me lie down in green pastures.
He leads me beside still waters.
He restores my soul.
He leads me in paths of righteousness for his name's sake.
Even though I walk through the valley of the
shadow of death, I will fear no evil,
For you are with me;
Your rod and Your staff, they comfort me.
You prepare a table before me in the presence of my enemies;
you anoint my head with oil;
My cup overflows.
Surely goodness and mercy shall follow me
All the days of my life,
And I shall dwell in the house of the Lord
Forever.

Background Discussion

- What stood out to you the most throughout this chapter?

- What are the major themes of Psalm 22, Psalm 23 & Psalm 24? How do they connect to one another?

- Who is the subject in Psalm 23?

- What is the result of trusting God, who is our Shepherd?

- What kinds of emotional trauma are blocking your trust in God?

- What does it look like to trust God in this coming week?

Chapter 1. The Lord is My Shepherd

"The Lord is My Shepherd"
Psalm 23:1a

Scripture for deeper study: John 10:1-18
ഗ‌ര

"This is indeed the pearl of the Psalms, a nightingale sings in the world's night of loneliness and need."
- Kale M. Yates[1]

"Psalm 23 is a poem with serene confession of trust, yet a poem with dynamic and powerful conviction about God as our Shepherd." Sang Kun Lee, The Lee's Commentary on The Psalms.[2]

Psa. 22 is the Good Shepherd dying for His sheep. (John. 10:11.) Psa. 23 is the Great Shepherd caring for His sheep. (Heb. 13:20.) Psa. 24 is the Chief Shepherd coming again for His sheep. (1 Pet. 5:4.)[3]

Many Christians can relate with King David's experiences as he went through life with deadly and traumatic events. There are numerous opinions by the scholars about the timing of when David might have written Psalm 23. Regardless, David had been through some dark times, perhaps after his sin with Bathsheba and the death of his baby as one of the darkest, but David continued to trust God with a strong conviction and hope that God prevails.

---

[1] Yates, Kyle M. Preaching from the Psalms. New York: Harper & Row, Publishers, 1948.
[2] Lee, Sang Kun. The Lee's commentary on the Psalms. Taegu Chikhalsi, Songdungsa, 1994.
[3] Brooks, Keith L. Summarized Bible: Complete Summary of the Old Testament. Bible Institute of Los Angeles, 1919.

One of the darkest struggles that a person may battle is their experience of sin.

> *for all have sinned and fall short of the glory of God (Romans 3:23)*

When those dark moments visit us, our faith may seem to shake around like hurricane, as if traveling in the valley of the shadow of death. However, in the midst of those moments, God's assurance of hope reveals a beam of light as he shows himself to us as a great Shepherd. Through these horrific situations, we can experience the merciful God, the only one who can lead us out of a dark time, out of the valley of the shadow of death and into God's glorious presence. The heart of God encourages the broken hearted.

> *"bruised reed he will not break, and a faintly burning wick he will not quench; he will faithfully bring forth justice." (Isaiah 42:3)*

Psalm 23 provides a picture of Jesus through the life experiences of David. In early ancient times, a king was often referred to as a shepherd.[4]

A strong focus in Psalm 23 is not always the sheep or a sheep's faith, but on the Shepherd, God Himself and God's sovereignty in His saving grace. There are about 15 verbs in Psalm 23:

God's Actions:
- Is (to be)
- Makes lie down
- Leads
- Restores
- Guides
- Are with
- Comforts

Our Response:
- Not be in Want
- Walk
- Overflow
- Dwell

---

[4] Merrill, Eugene H. (2008) *Kingdom of priests: a history of Old Testament Israel.* Grand Rapids, MI, Baker Academic.

- Anoints
- Overflows
- Follow
- Prepares

God reveals ways that we can trust Him by intentionally observing these 15 action verbs.

A theme of Psalm 23 is "trust," trusting God who is our Shepherd. Trust is a loaded word in a broken society. We experience disappointment from our parents, significant others, children, family and friends. Our vulnerability is balanced by implementing healthy boundaries in our relationships. However, our relationship with God is unique because *he will never leave us* (Hebrews 13:5).

Part I. Shepherds

*I*n modern times, especially from a western cultural perspective, if you have not been exposed to raising sheep, the perspective we may have of a shepherd is a warm and cozy figure similar to the illustration of Jesus lovingly and gently holding the little lamb. However, when the Bible mentions a shepherd, applying a historical context reveals more depth and attributes that we desire to strive towards.

The Bible uses the illustration of a shepherd and sheep on many occasions; the shepherd held a position of authority over his sheep and would fight to protect the sheep from any invaders, elements or beings who might threaten the sheep. The sheep greatly admire and revere their shepherd.

However, to other people, a shepherd was considered one of the lowliest persons in human society. Their testimony was not even valid in court, yet a shepherd is exactly whom God used to first announce to mankind that the Messiah was born in a manger in Bethlehem. A shepherd is also a title that God uses to refer to Himself. A shepherd is a role that we all take on when we bear an influence on another person such as parent on child, teacher on student, mentor on mentee, or peer on peer.

The definition of shepherd as defined by Strongs:

> 7462. רָעָה râ'âh, raw-aw'; a prim. root; to tend a flock, i.e. pasture it; intrans. to graze (lit.) or fig.); gen. to rule; by extens. to associate with (as a friend):—× break, companion, keep company with, devour, eat up, evil entreat, feed, use as a friend, make friendship with, herdman, keep [sheep] (-er), pastor, + shearing house, shepherd, wander, waste.[5]

This word is used about 150 times in the Old Testament. The word, shepherd, was used for the first time in Genesis 4:2, where Able was a keeper of sheep.

> "Shepherd" is never a title explicitly used of a king in Israel, but God appoints kings to shepherd His people, Israel. This includes David and his lineage (2 Sam 5:2; 1 Chr 11:2; Psa 78:70–72; Ezek 34:23; 37:24)[6]

> The task of the shepherd was described as follow; The task of the shepherd was to care for the flock, to find grass and water, to protect it from wild animals (Am 3:12), to look for and restore those that strayed (Ez 34:8; Mt 18:12), to lead the flock out each day going before it and to return the flock at the close of the day to the fold (Jn 10:2–4). At times, the shepherd led the flock far from home and sheltered the animals by night in a cave or sheepfold built of field stones; he would lie across the entrance. The

[5] Strong, J. (1995). New Strongs exhaustive concordance of the Bible: With main concordance, appendix to the main concordance, Hebrew and Aramaic dictionary of the Old Testament, Greek dictionary of the New Testament. Nashville, TN: Thomas Nelson.

[6] Barry, J. D., Bomar, D., Brown, D. R., Klippenstein, R., Mangum, D., Sinclair Wolcott, C., … Widder, W. (Eds.). (2016). In The Lexham Bible Dictionary. Bellingham, WA: Lexham Press.

shepherd was responsible to the owner for every sheep and was required to make restitution for losses (Gn 31:39; Ex 22:10–13). Shepherds and their flocks enjoyed a close relationship (2 Sm 12:3; Jn 10:3, 4) giving them constant care (Ez 34:4, 5; Mt 9:36; 26:31).[7]

The main role of a shepherd is to feed, guide, tend and protect their sheep. Further analysis of a Shepherd's role can be seen when Jesus challenges and commissions Peter to *"feed my lambs, tend my sheep, and feed my sheep"* in John 21:15-17.

Part II. The Shepherd

When we see David's life, we can see a glimpse of a fearless shepherd in 1 Samuel 17:33-37. Before the giant Goliath, the young David submitted his resume to Saul who had doubts because David was young and seemed inexperienced, but David knew the God of Israel would be with him in this battle as God had been with him when he was rescuing his sheep from lions and bears.

> *And David said, "The LORD who delivered me from the paw of the lion and from the paw of the bear will deliver me from the hand of this Philistine." And Saul said to David, "Go, and the LORD be with you!" (1 Samuel 17:37)*

God was with David and David had the first victory among Israel. Psalm 78:70-72 described David as following; *He chose David his servant and took him from the sheepfolds; from following the nursing ewes he brought him to shepherd Jacob his people, Israel his inheritance. With upright heart he shepherded them and guided them with his skillful hand.*

We see Jesus as the Good Shepherd in John 10 and Matthew 18:10-14. As we read John 10, the concept of a good shepherd who loves and cares for

---

[7] Elwell, W. A., & Beitzel, B. J. (1988). In Baker encyclopedia of the Bible. Grand Rapids, MI: Baker Book House.

us comes alive with hope when we are caught in the midst of chaos in a hostile world. In America, we have the privilege to walk in the freedom of living out our faith and we walk in that faith, trusting in God as a Good Shepherd who cares for our well-being. I was again thanking God for the freedom we have by living in America. We can be safely shepherded by God's sovereignty, His mercy and grace.

> *I am the good shepherd. The good shepherd lays down his life for the sheep. He who is a hired hand and not a shepherd, who does not own the sheep, sees the wolf coming and leaves the sheep and flees, and the wolf snatches them and scatters them. He flees because he is a hired hand and cares nothing for the sheep. I am the good shepherd. I know my own and my own know me, just as the Father knows me and I know the Father; and I lay down my life for the sheep. (John 10:11-15)*

The good shepherd is one who loves people so well, that they lay down their life and desires for others. However, there is also an enemy that seeks to destroy God's people, yet God continues to pursue us to draw us close to the heart of God.

> *The thief comes only to steal and kill and destroy. I came that they may have life and have it abundantly. I am the good shepherd. The good shepherd lays down his life for the sheep. (John 10:10-11)*

> *If a man has a hundred sheep, and one of them has gone astray, does he not leave the ninety-nine on the mountains and go in search of the one that went astray? And if he finds it, truly, I say to you, he rejoices over it more than over the ninety-nine that never went astray. So it is not the will of my Father who is in heaven that one of these little ones should perish. (Matthew 18:10-14)*

There are incredible descriptions about Jesus as a shepherd in the New Testament. It is a description that we all yearn for, a shepherd who loves us enough to die to protect and save us. There is not much to say other than read those scriptures and follow the steps of Jesus. The truth in John 10 is a declaration for anyone who seeks to love and disciple others as God commissions us in Matthew 28:18-20, but we must pursue and recognize the authority and will of the Chief Shepherd, Jesus.

Knowing and understanding the role of shepherds, which is exemplified by Jesus, gives us, as leaders, the desire to guide sheep with tenderness, yet with a blazing, protective heart for sheep. Jeremiah witnessed the devastating days when Israel did not have a good shepherd to lead them in God's ways. The results lead to the nation of Israel being exiled to Babylon. Often, we focus on seeking grace, yet dismiss the justice against the injustice that harmed our flocks. We need more shepherds who can stand up for our faith, not to bring legalistic Christian culture, but to protect and raise our sheep.

Part III. Good Shepherd

Luke 15:1-7 describes well about the shepherd who is after a lost sheep.

> *A painter, Alford Usher Soord (1868-1915) painted The Parable of The Lost Sheep, which depicts a shepherd hanging on the edge of a cliff, leaning over to rescue a lost sheep who is stranded on this perilous cliff, yet the shepherd fearlessly reaches out, risking his own life to save the precious sheep.*[8]

This painting is a beautiful picture of the ministry of loving people who have experienced abortion or great loss, who need loving hands to come alongside. Also, the painting is a gentle picture of bringing God's truth in love as God is the ultimate rescuer and healer. A major role of the

---

[8] http://transformationsandwhispers.blogspot.com

shepherds is to seek out the lost sheep who are entangled in the briars of pain and suffering.

When it comes to shepherds and tending sheep, there is a Chief Shepherd, or The Shepherd who oversees the flock. However, they usually have under shepherds who follow the wise guidance of the Chief Shepherd in caring and guiding the sheep. Jesus is our Chief Shepherd. When caring for the sheep, the Chief Shepherd will often take a vantage point where they can see the whole landscape and direct the under shepherds to where the next meal might be or where a good food and safe water source is located or what direction should be taken to find rest. This Chief Shepherd plays a critical role in the health and safety of both the under shepherds and the sheep.

God also commended His people to be 'a good under shepherd' by feeding the sheep with good nutrition, timely food and protecting the sheep in times of difficulty. (Matthew 24:45, Luke 12:42)

By learning God's character, we can learn to experience <u>rest in and trust</u> the Good Shepherd. As we live in a time with rapidly advancing technology, we tend to be overloaded with information, and exposed to so many things which are vying for our attention and resources. This includes a variety of good things, evil things and unimportant things. We can be overwhelmed with the responsibility of righting the injustice overflowing all around us. However, by knowing God is our Good Shepherd, we can rest in Him by trusting Him. None of the things that happen are a surprise to God and He already has a battle plan drawn out with a promise– ultimate victory that will come to pass. Until then, it is our responsibility to make disciples, guarding them against the pervasive lies, and building them up so that they can make their own disciples as God commanded in Matthew 28:18-20.

During one of those dark times where grief and pain had overcome Israel due to their exile to Babylon, Jeremiah shared hope to the Israelites:

The steadfast love of the Lord never ceases; his mercies never come to an end; they are new every morning; great is your faithfulness. (Lamentations 3:22-23)

Our Good Shepherd is faithful to walk with us in all seasons, meeting us exactly where we are at.

Walter Kaiser stated: *No wonder this phrase, 'Great is Thy faithfulness', springs from the page as the greatest word of hope. But it was not sung* (as we so often sing the hymn based on this verse) *immediately after the body of believers had just experienced another evidence of God's blessing on their lives. On the contrary, this word came when nothing looked possible, hopeful, worthwhile, or comforting.*

In the face of the direst of adversities, Israel and we are offered hope. It is a word not about answers to the problem of evil; not a word about circumstances or men and movements. It is not a word about systems of political or even theological belief; it is simply a word about our Lord. He is faithful, He is love, He is gracious, He is full of compassion, He is our inheritance.[9]

As the painting by Alford Soord illustrates, may God grant each of us the heart of a shepherd. The heart of one who seeks out the lost sheep who are wounded and hurting and brings them to restoration. Let's praise God for his goodness and faithfulness that he lavishes upon us as our Good Shepherd.

಼ಎ ಞ

Jehovah-rohi, God is my Shepherd

---

[9] Walter C. Kaiser, Jr., Grief and Pain in the Plan of God Christian Assurance and the Message of Lamentations. Christian Focus, 2004.

Psalm 23:1a Discussion

- What stood out to you the most through this chapter?

- Who is the ultimate Shepherd in our lives?

- What is the character of Jesus as the Good Shepherd in John 10 and Matthew 18:14?

- What does God say about the shepherd who was not faithful in Jeremiah 23 and Ezekiel 34 during the time of the fall of Jerusalem?

- What should be the character of a shepherd as a leader and a follower of Jesus?

- Why do people enter an abortion clinic? What may be their concerns or state of mind?

- How should a good and trained shepherd approach those who have experienced abortion or any other traumatic circumstances?

Chapter 2. I Shall Not Want

"I shall not want."
Psalm 23:1b

Scripture for deeper study: Matthew 6:19-34

ଥ ଓ

We live in a society where we are bombarded from every direction with enticing advertisements on TV, internet, in stores and magazines exclaiming why we absolutely need this or that to have fulfillment in life. I remember a few years back, there was a Super Bowl commercial that was advertising a car as something that will bring us joy. I am learning that joy is something that is external to our happiness. Happiness is but a mere temporary feeling based on circumstances. Joy on the other hand is not dependent on feelings, but is a state of resting in peace and contentment. Jesus is sitting on the throne, nothing surprises him and regardless of circumstances, in our hearts, we can say with confidence *"the joy of the LORD is my strength." (Nehemiah 8:10b)*

Part I: Desires

Each of us have desires, sometimes great and overwhelming and sometimes petty and insignificant while other times they are simple and unobtrusive. Oftentimes these desires stem from personal looks, the car we drive, monetary status or power, our health, our family's safety, forgiveness, freedom, independence, marital status and relationships and the list goes on...

However, the number one desire that we should be concerned about is the wellbeing of our internal inmost being, which can be fulfilled through our personal relationship with God.

Delight yourself in the Lord, and he will give you the desires of your heart. (Psalm 37:4)

And this is the confidence that we have toward him, that if we ask anything according to his will he hears us. (1 John 5:14)

These precious promises may often be used out of context, so it is important to draw close to God and to know His heart. We want to share in the same desires and heart attitudes that God has. That is not to say that God does not want to give you what you desire.

Every good gift and every perfect gift is from above, coming down from the Father of lights, with whom there is no variation or shadow due to change. (James 1:17)

God has hand crafted you and gifted you with a unique set of passions, desires, abilities and opportunities to grow and serve in your relationship with God and others. Throughout the book of Deuteronomy, after God had sent the mighty plagues to rescue the people of Israel from Egypt, God's plea with them was to remember. Remember how great and reliable God is! How He provided for their every need, including their food, water, the clothes on their backs and the sandals on their feet never wore out throughout the 40 years in the desert!

"And now, Israel, what does the LORD your God require of you, but to fear the LORD your God, to walk in all his ways, to love him, to serve the LORD your God with all your heart and with all your soul, and to keep the commandments and statutes of the LORD, which I am commanding you today for your good? (Deuteronomy 10:12-13)

God's one request of Israel, his ambassador and priest to all the nations of the world is quoted repeatedly by Jesus in the gospels:

And he [Jesus] said to him, "You shall love the LORD your God with all your heart and with all your soul and with all your mind." (Matthew 22:37)

You shall love the LORD your God with all your heart and with all your soul and with all your might. (Deuteronomy 6:5)

Joshua echoes the commands that God gave Moses to relay to the people, noting that the desires of our heart should be aligned with God's desires.

Only be very careful to observe the commandment and the law that Moses the servant of the Lord commanded you, to love the Lord your God, and to walk in all his ways and to keep his commandments and to cling to him and to serve him with all your heart and with all your soul. (Joshua 22:5)

So our very first focus is to align ourselves with God's heart desires. And what is it that He desires? Obedience by loving God and people. Love is a verb and action.

Love is patient and kind; love does not envy or boast; it is not arrogant or rude. It does not insist on its own way; it is not irritable or resentful; it does not rejoice at wrongdoing, but rejoices with the truth. Love bears all things, believes all things, hopes all things, endures all things. (1 Corinthians 13:4-7)

So often we glide over these words that sound so nice, especially at weddings. These actions of love, to put others first, to be intentional, to keep no record of the wrongs against you, to truly *let it go* and give it to God, not holding a grudge, but to forgive. Maybe it was a wrong done against you, maybe you are struggling to forgive yourself. When we dwell on the desires of self, we are missing out on the blessings that God wants to bestow. We get to choose who we want to author our desires. There is so much joy when we lay down our own selfish desires, in favor of God's desires.

Part II: Decisions

*F*oMo – the "Fear Of Missing Out" is a new condition of anxiety that is facing our upcoming generations with the influx of social media. We can see all the fun things that everyone is doing and desire to be connected. However, this focus shifts us from looking at the ultimate truth in God and His kingdom. Instead we may look to ourselves, other people or the desire to find fulfillment in other things, whether that is other people, addictions, shows or food and the list goes on. When we are absorbed with the world's attractions, then we miss out on the richness of the Good Shepherd's abundant life.

> *Do not be anxious about anything, but in everything by prayer and supplication with thanksgiving let your requests be made known to God. And the peace of God, which surpasses all understanding, will guard your hearts and your minds in Christ Jesus. (Philippians 4:6-8)*

We do not always make the best decisions, but the consequences still come, whether they are positive or less favorable. Our past can influence how we will act in the present, which influences the situations we find ourselves in the future.

However, we should not dwell on our yesterday. Yesterday is gone and tomorrow is not yet here. What we have control over is the present – an infinitely small piece of time that is constantly transitioning from future to present and then quickly becomes history.

Both Joshua and Elijah sent out a call to arms to the people of Israel, they witnessed God doing amazing things and followed the Shepherd. Joshua had finished leading the people to victory by inhabiting the promised land. He then challenged the people individually and corporately with their relationship with God.

> But if you refuse to serve the Lord, then choose today whom you will serve. Would you prefer the gods your ancestors served beyond the Euphrates? Or will it be the gods of the Amorites in whose land you now live? But as for me and my family, we will serve the LORD." (Joshua 24:15 NLT)

> The people said to Joshua, "We will serve the LORD our God. We will obey him alone." (Joshua 24:24 NLT)

Israel decided to follow God. However, a few generations later, the people of Israel were so lost and forgot their promise and decision to follow God. Thankfully, God is so gracious! He sent the prophet Elijah to relay God's heart and desires to the people.

> Then Elijah stood in front of them and said, "How much longer will you waver, hobbling between two opinions? If the LORD is God, follow him! But if Baal is God, then follow him!" But the people were completely silent. (1 Kings 18:21 NLT)

The people of Israel were so lost that they did not even know how to choose. Sometimes we can feel overwhelmed in our circumstances. The Israelites were surrounded by all kinds of idols and forms of worship that they no longer knew right and wrong or which god to choose. Elijah stood steadfast in this epic showdown and God showed up in a great and mighty way!

> O Lord, answer me! Answer me so these people will know that you, O LORD, are God and that you have brought them back to yourself." Immediately the fire of the LORD flashed down from heaven and burned up the young bull,

the wood, the stones, and the dust. It even licked up all the water in the trench! And when all the people saw it, they fell face down on the ground and cried out, "The LORD— he is God! Yes, the LORD is God!" (1 Kings 18:37-39 NLT)

We may not personally witness God answering by fire, but we have numerous testaments of God's awesomeness because we have the witnesses of who God is: in written form in the Bible, His creation, the testimony of what God has done and is doing in our life, and the lives of those around us.

Elijah, the heroes in the Bible and the disciples in the New Testament made the decision to follow God, to lay down their own desires in favor of pursuing God and His glorious Kingdom. As we experience the testimonies of God at work in our personal life, we witness ourselves being transformed as our desires shift from self-centeredness to serving others.

And he said to all, "If anyone would come after me, let him deny himself and take up his cross daily and follow me. (Luke 9:23)

This is our act of obedience – to daily put down our personal desires and put on the character of the Spirit of *love, joy, peace, patience, kindness, goodness, faithfulness, gentleness and self-control (Galatians 5:22-23)* as we walk in obedience to God to *love Him first and love others* (Luke 10:27).

A special blessing that Jesus expressed to Thomas, the disciple who needed to see Jesus to believe that He had risen to life after death, encourages me in my adventures with God, of loving Him and the people in my life.

Jesus said to him, "Have you believed because you have seen me? Blessed are those who have not seen and yet have believed." (John 20:29)

The decision to follow God is not always easy in this world, but it comes with a reward and impact that lasts for all eternity.

Part III: Contentment

Sheep do not have to worry about wanting anything because the shepherd sees to all their needs. They can enjoy spending time with the shepherd without the distraction of worry or anticipation. The shepherd provides exactly what they need and when they need it.

> *"Therefore I tell you, do not be anxious about your life, what you will eat or what you will drink, nor about your body, what you will put on. Is not life more than food, and the body more than clothing? 26 Look at the birds of the air: they neither sow nor reap nor gather into barns, and yet your heavenly Father feeds them. Are you not of more value than they? 27 And which of you by being anxious can add a single hour to his span of life? (Matthew 6:25-27)*

> *But seek first his kingdom and his righteousness, and all these things will be given to you as well. Therefore do not worry about tomorrow, for tomorrow will worry about itself. Each day has enough trouble of its own." (Matthew 6:33-34 NLT)*

Worry not and fear not because God is constantly at work in and through our life as we allow Him to be!

> We are encouraged to *Be relaxed with what you have. Since God assured us, "I'll never let you down, never walk off and leave you," we can boldly quote, God is there, ready to help; I'm fearless no matter what. Who or what can get to me? (Hebrews 13:5 MSG)*

We can live full lives and embrace the present, trusting the Good Shepherd who has our best interests at heart. He is weaving together an exquisite story throughout our life that reflects the greatness, goodness and beauty of God and connects to God's greater story of His Mighty Kingdom that is to come. He is also our redeemer and constantly redeeming every difficult thing, transforming all the painful things of our lives into wondrous & beautiful ways we would never have imagined. He works all things for good despite what the circumstances might look like in the moment as seen in Romans 8:28. We see in Genesis 45:7, after Joseph was sold into slavery by his brothers, but God used the tragedy to place Joseph in a position of authority that would save many nations and people from the great famine that lasted 7 years.

Joseph of the Old Testament believed God and put on a heart attitude of trust and contentment. Paul, one of the early and most influential disciples of Jesus, a man who had everything this world had to offer in the first century: wealth, prominence, education and citizenship, counted it all as rubbish in favor of knowing Christ. He summed up the heart attitude of joy and contentment.

> *Not that I was ever in need, for I have learned how to be content with whatever I have. I know how to live on almost nothing or with everything. I have learned the secret of living in every situation, whether it is with a full stomach or empty, with plenty or little. For I can do everything through Christ, who gives me strength. (Philippians 4:11-13 NLT)*

Paul chose to follow the Good Shepherd, pursuing God's Kingdom and walking confidently in Christ, constantly examining himself to see if he was walking in obedience, laying down his desires in favor of God's desires.

Despite difficult circumstances, we can still say with confidence, "I shall not want." The meaning of "I shall not want" can come from the experience of heavenly things that do not exist on earth, but lead us to place one's fulfilled with the affection of our Heavenly Father.

In Greek, the word, "want", has another meaning; that is "lack". Therefore, I lack nothing. This does not mean we will have everything we want and need, rather we will experience that we lack nothing because of the presence of God as our shepherd. The word, "lack" was also used in Exodus while Israel was in the wilderness for 40 years through the Moses' leadership in Deuteronomy 2:7.[10]

When the Israelites wandered the desert, God provided for them with exactly what they needed, with perfect timing and portions. He provided longevity for their clothes and shoes which did not wear out for forty years. For nutrition, God provided the people with daily bread called "manna", meat would fall out of the sky and water would gush out of rocks to satisfy the thirst for over a million people (Exodus 12:37).

Depending on our worldview and understanding of the Bible, our spiritual appetite may vary. When we pursue the things of this world, we seem to always be lacking something because we will never have enough. However, when we pursue Heavenly matters, we will lack nothing because God will provide everything we need according to His glorious riches.

While we are living in this world, as humans, we are already at war with our sinful flesh and will have desires and cravings for this world. No one is exempt from such a state until God calls us home to heaven. However, by living and experiencing the emptiness of this world, the contrasting glory of God's love and living life with Him and for Him is transformational. As with plants, whatever is nurtured will grow and blossom. If we give in to the desires of the flesh, then we will deteriorate. However, when we feed the spirit through spending time with God, studying His word, loving people well, going to war in prayer and sharing the abundant life and freedom in Christ, then the spirit will be stronger and the richness of our relationships with God and others that much richer.

---

[10] Bullock, C. Hassell, et al. Psalms. Baker Books, 2015.

No matter what difficulties we may face, we can walk in confidence that God walks with us, transforming our future while He is redeeming our past.

> *Today I have given you the choice between life and death, between blessings and curses. Now I call on heaven and earth to witness the choice you make. Oh, that you would choose life, so that you and your descendants might live! (Deuteronomy 30:19 NLT)*

May we choose to live life abundantly, rest in God and His promises, living in a heart attitude of contentment.

୫୦୧୫

El Roi, the God who sees me

Psalm 23:1b Discussion

- What stood out to you the most throughout this chapter?

- What are some of the greatest desires of your heart in this season of life?

- What are some of the greatest desires of God's heart for your life?

- What areas of your life have you withheld from God?

- Are you currently living in the past, the present, or the future? If this needs to be changed, how does it need to be changed?

- In what areas of your life is God asking you to surrender to allow Him to work?

- How do you pursue God when you are making decisions? Do you include him in every decision you make?

- What does it look like to live a life of contentment? How do we live our daily lives, walking in a joy of satisfaction that is external to our emotional circumstances?

Chapter 3. Green Pastures

"He makes me lie down in green pastures."
Psalm 23:2a

Scripture for deeper study: Isaiah 40:27-31
ഇൽ

*H*ave you been hungry? Or have you seen hungry children?

When we are hungry, we become short tempered, weary ill-mannered, unkind and easily irritated until our hunger is satisfied.

Sheep are the same way.

As humans, we may recognize the experience of physical hunger, but our being must also be maintained emotionally, mentally and spiritually to sustain a healthy body and lifestyle.

We live in a highly health–conscious generation: from food, medicine, cosmetics and recreation, advertisements, reviews, plans and help-guides are everywhere and can be overwhelming.

We can compare the symptoms of our physical condition with the symptoms of our spiritual well-being, whether we are practicing a weak diet or eating well. Stepping back and reflecting on our cultural influence, personal habits and lifestyles, we gain perspective and understanding about our spiritual condition, and can reexamine where we want our health to be and how to make that happen. Let's examine our understanding of sheep at a deeper level to tend them wisely.

Part I. Character of Sheep

*T*he definition of sheep is as follows:

> *Sheep: The Hebrew terms for sheep are:* צֹאן *tson, a flock of sheep;* שֶׂה *seh, a single sheep or goat;* אַיִל *ayil, a ram;* רָכֵל *rakal, a ewe;* כֶּבֶשׂ *kebes, fem.* כִּבְשָׂה *kebesah, a young sheep of over a year;* טָלֶה *taleh, a sucking lamb;* כַּר *kar, a lamb in the pasture.*[11]

The words related to sheep are mentioned about 700 times. There are many positive, negative, and sometimes embarrassing connections between the nature of people and the precious sheep.

When sheep are experiencing fear, anxiety, uncertainty or even feeling unsafe, the sheep will refuse to lie down in the pasture. The sheep must be feeling perfectly safe and content for the sheep to lay down and relax. Sometimes, because the Shepherds will lovingly force resistant sheep to the ground so that the sheep will lay down and rest.

> According to Dr. Vernon McGee in his book Psalms, he said, *not only do sheep need safety, they need sufficiency and satisfaction. "He maketh me to lie down in green pastures." That is sufficiency. Folks that know sheep tell us that a hungry sheep will not lie down. When sheep are lying down in green pastures, it means they have their tummies full. And Christ is our sufficiency. "Jesus said unto them, I am the bread of life: he that cometh to me shall never hunger; and he that believeth on me shall never thirst." (John 6:35)*[12]

---

[11] Hart, Henry Chichester. Scripture Natural History. II. The Animals Mentioned in the Bible. Religious Tract Society, 1888.

[12] McGee, Vernon J., and McGee, J. Vernon. Thru the Bible Commentary: Psalms 2 18. United States of America, Thomas Nelson, 1997.

Jesus told them this story: "If a man has a hundred sheep and one of them gets lost, what will he do? Won't he leave the ninety-nine others in the wilderness and go to search for the one that is lost until he finds it? And when he has found it, he will joyfully carry it home on his shoulders. When he arrives, he will call together his friends and neighbors, saying, 'Rejoice with me because I have found my lost sheep.' In the same way, there is more joy in heaven over one lost sinner who repents and returns to God than over ninety-nine others who are righteous and haven't strayed away! (Luke 15:3-7 NLT)

The story is also repeated in the Gospel of Matthew 18:12-14. How marvelous that God's love is! His love is so deep that he pursues and draws us and creation back to himself. No matter how far lost we have wandered or unprotected in the enemy's territory, we are never too far to return to God's household. And upon return, how greatly we celebrate being restored!

But while he was still a long way off, his father saw him and felt compassion, and ran and embraced him and kissed him. And the son said to him, 'Father, I have sinned against heaven and before you. I am no longer worthy to be called your son.' But the father said to his servants, 'Bring quickly the best robe, and put it on him, and put a ring on his hand, and shoes on his feet. And bring the fattened calf and kill it, and let us eat and celebrate. For this my son was dead, and is alive again; he was lost, and is found.' And they began to celebrate. (Luke 15:20b-24)

According to Phillip Keller in his book, A Shepherd Looks at Psalm 23,

"The strange thing about sheep is that because of their very make-up it is almost impossible for them to be made to lie down unless four requirements are met.

Owing to their timidity they refuse to lie down unless they are free of all fear. Because of the social behavior within a flock, sheep will not lie down unless they are free from friction with others of their kind. If tormented by flies or parasites sheep will not lie down. Only when free of these pests can they relax. Lastly, sheep will not lie down as long as they feel in need of finding food. They must free from hunger.

It is significant that to be at rest must be a definite sense of freedom from fear, tension, aggravation, and hunger. The unique aspect of the picture is that it is only the sheep man himself who can provide release from these anxieties. It all depends upon the diligence of the owner whether or not his flock is free of disturbing influences.[13]

Look around and what do we see? Hurting people looking for the same safety. When we apply these aspects to those who experienced abortion, we can have a glimpse of how we approach the matter of abortion among the flock. After experiencing a trauma, we are often scared, paranoid and untrusting because the pains have left them in a very vulnerable position. When we choose to care for precious sheep, we want to be intentional in creating a safe, loving environment where the sheep can rest and find healing.

As finite humans, we are trying to figure out the social problem, yet we are witnessing the consequences of imperfect human plans and systems. Every election season, there are numerous plans and promises that seems to be the solution for all of humanity. In a fallen world, the problems that plague humanity will never be completely banished. God knows we need shepherds. Jesus' last words and commissioning for Peter was to "*feed my lambs, tend my sheep, and feed my sheep*" in John 21:15-17. This is how we show our love for God – by seeing to the needs of the young ones, helping them to grow and teaching them the things of God.

---

[13] Keller, W. Phillip. A Shepherd Looks at Psalm 23. Zondervan, 2015.

When we think of sheep, we tend to picture a cute little lamb, maybe in the crook of Jesus' arms, however, sheep are also not the brightest animals. They require an intentional, loving shepherd to keep watch over them because they often stumble, wander off and do very foolish things.

Sheep need guidance; sheep need shepherds.

Sheep require very purposeful attention to every detail of their living environment. They need to be provided with proper nutrition in a timely manner. In the same way, we as sheep are bombarded with information and we must learn how to filter everything that we learn, hear and read. Without a proper filter and lens to translate and understand all the things that are happening to and around us, we can be easily lost or confused. It is important to seek and find a healthy community of people who are striving together towards the truth and reality as given by God. This also means asking God to bring you to good under-shepherds, teachers, pastors, mentors or disciple makers – whichever term you prefer – who are likeminded – mature in their relationship with God, who will walk with you in this season of healing and growing into maturity.

As we grow into maturity, we may feel under-qualified to walk alongside others, but God equips us for the work that he has set before us.

> *And God is able to make all grace abound to you, so that having all sufficiency in all things at all times, you may abound in every good work. (2 Corinthians 9:8)*

Living as a shepherd's role in someone's life can be intimidating, but eternally rewarding. There will be difficult times, there will be frustration, and also there will be joys and celebrations! Hopefully, there will also be a lot of self-reflection and learning as we try to figure out how to best communicate God's truth in a way that the receiver will understand. We all learn and interpret things differently, so when we are communicating and loving others, it is important to be intentional to connect things in a way that they will understand.

> *Now may the God of peace—who brought up from the dead our Lord Jesus, the great Shepherd of the sheep and ratified an eternal covenant with his blood—may he equip you with all you need for doing his will.*
> *May he produce in you, through the power of Jesus Christ, every good thing that is pleasing to him.*
> *All glory to him forever and ever! Amen.*
> *(Hebrews 13:20-21 NLT)*

When we witness the hands of God moving in each person's life, we cannot deny the truth in the Bible because what happened in the early church is still happening today. God is still at work, encouraging us, building us up and meeting our needs individually and collectively. Even if a lost sheep bites back as we are tending it, recognizing that the sheep is just scared and uncertain of a new sheepfold. As a shepherd, persevering in this kind relationship opens up the opportunity for healing and blessing.

Within the sheep and shepherd relationship, there will be moments when the sheep understands, the "ah ha" moment when everything seems to come together! That is one of the sweetest and most awesome experiences because a precious sheep experienced a victory in their journey of healing.

Part II. Green Pastures

I was a mess with a combination of having had an abortion, a legalistic background with no room for error and an unhealthy spiritual diet, stuffed with anything related to Jesus that I could find, but without any guidance to understand what I was reading and hearing. As I was continually fed by healthy churches, strong classes and people who are solidly rooted in Jesus, I was able to transition and began settling down (metaphorical expression as a sheep) with the right understanding of the scriptures.

Studying the Bible can be compared to swimming, snorkeling, or scuba diving to describe the impact of the adventure of getting into God's word. If we study a little deeper into John 21:1-17, we can see a clearer picture about what Jesus is commissioning Peter to do.
There are three times Jesus told Peter to feed His sheep.

Peter's first role commissioned by Jesus was "feeding" in John 21:15-17.

In Jesus' commission to Peter in John 21:15-17, Jesus asks Peter three times if Peter loves Him. Peter gets slightly offended that Jesus is questioning his love, but Jesus responds with a different response for Peter after each affirmation of Peter's love for Jesus. The first time, Jesus responds with *feed my lambs*, the second time *tend my sheep*, the third time, *feed my sheep*.

Our English interpretations of the Bible use slightly different word choices of feed and tend to express how Peter as an under-shepherd is to lead his sheep. This is a high calling to look after the needs of the sheep, not restricted to physical food, but all areas of the sheep's life. From birth to maturity, with food, nutrition, wants and needs, the sheep need to be cared for with love.

We can see the context of Jesus' conversation and commissioning of Peter in John 21. Jesus had already died and was raised back to life and shown Himself very much alive to many. Meanwhile, Peter and a few of the disciples had returned to fishing, the family trade. Jesus meets them on the beach and performs a miracle of catching a huge load of fish, reminiscent of how they first met in Luke 5:1-11. Jesus then proceeds to feed the disciples the fish that were just caught along with some bread.

> *Jesus said to them, "Come and have breakfast." Now none of the disciples dared ask him, "Who are you?" They knew it was the Lord. Jesus came and took the bread and gave*

it to them, and so with the fish. This was now the third time that Jesus was revealed to the disciples after he was raised from the dead. (John 21:12-14)

This was one of the last times that the disciples were able to meet with Jesus in person. He had a plan for these disciples, to *feed my lambs, tend my sheep*, and to *feed my sheep*. They were not to remain as fishermen but rather to *Follow Jesus* and be *fishers of men* Matthew 4:19. These were the words that Jesus left with the disciples whom He had spent so much time with and has given to us as well, *Follow Me* and *take care of my flock*.

When we look to God as our Shepherd, we can be blissfully content because God sees to our every need, so we can say "*I shall not want*." This is followed by "*He makes me lie down in green pastures,*" which indicates that the sheep have found peace and healing. However, there are many barriers to us sheep adhering to fearless rest. We live in a culture that addresses many heart issues, including abortion as a taboo conversation, making it difficult to work through our emotions and pain. So after burying pain and going further into destructive lifestyle, instead of cleansing, we may find ourselves in deeper sinking sand that prevents the healing process. We arrive at the point of desperately needing a savior. We are hungry to hear the truth and hope of God's Kingdom. We require God's truth, identity and power to wash us clean, to give us a heart of peace.

A good shepherd will lead the sheep to healthy food that is nutritious, because as sheep, there is a lot of food that looks like it is good for food, but it is poisonous and will reap a bad stomachache, disease or even death. What we eat and allow into our bodies will influence our overall health. There are things in the world that our flesh desires, but it is not good for us. Spiritual food works in a similar way. We must decide if we want to eat the food provided by the Good Shepherd or the food we find while wandering.

> "*All things are lawful for me,*" but not all things are helpful. "*All things are lawful for me,*" but I will not be dominated by anything. (1 Corinthians 6:12)

The Good Shepherd is also so gracious because he will gently pick up each sheep and wash them carefully, addressing their hurts and pains, exposing the lies that have clung to the sheep's wool to illuminate God's truth and our identity as a precious child of the King of Kings.

Part III. Experience Healing

I learned that it is extremely valuable to understand how to read the Bible. What is the context? Who is the audience? What is the cultural background and influence? Whom is God talking to? How did the audience interpret the situation? We cannot apply everything in the Bible in every circumstance without recognizing these important variables. If we try to self-diagnose by picking and choosing which verses sound good in the moment, then it could be likened to going to the doctor and telling him what prescription you need. Let's dive a little deeper into understanding Jesus.

> *In the beginning was the Word, and the Word was with God, and the Word was God. He was in the beginning with God. All things were made through him, and without him was not any thing made that was made. In him was life, and the life was the light of men. The light shines in the darkness, and the darkness has not overcome it. (1 John 1:1-5)*

Jesus is "the Word", "logos" in John 1:1. With the Word, He created us. The Word is the substance of who God is and He is the one who sustains and trains us. He also equips us to understand what God says through the Holy Spirit who lives within us when we make the decision to follow God. Without the Word, we will wither and die. In America, God's word is easily accessible through so many mediums: books in every form, the internet, tv, radio, apps, churches, podcasts, people, etc. We are extremely blessed to have so many resources available. The challenge is how to use those resources, and as sheep, we may confuse ourselves by seeking answers from unwise sources.

A metaphor can be seen from a doctor's visit. A person may interpret their simple cough to be a life threatening, rare disease after looking up the symptoms on an internet search. Then the patient tells the doctor that they are now dying and need a certain medication. Then the doctor has the challenge of calming the patient down and explaining why they do not have a life-threatening disease, and instead, they just have a cold and need to rest for a couple days.

> *And when Jesus heard it, he said to them, "Those who are well have no need of a physician, but those who are sick. I came not to call the righteous, but sinners." (Mark 2:17)*

If you are a sheep without a shepherd, you need protection. Find a church where you can get fed with the Word of God, living in a community of like-minded people so that you may get well. Give yourself grace in the forgiving process. Let God do the healing in your heart in his right timing by seeking him.

When meeting with hurting people, assumption is the enemy. Each situation is unique, and decisions are made because it seemed like the best idea at the time. The price of forgiveness was paid for in full by the life of God's Son, Jesus Christ. Let's think about it deeply. Forgiveness is not a casual subject to talk about without consideration.

Those who abuse others, do so out of selfishness for power and control. The abused struggle with confusing guilt, shame and other pain. Forgiving an abuser does not discount what was done but entrusts God with the outcome and repercussions of the injustice to God's righteous judgement. We are regaining the authority over our emotions, heart and mind by relinquishing our right of seeking vengeance and giving it over to God.

> *Beloved, never avenge yourselves, but leave it to the wrath of God, for it is written, "Vengeance is mine, I will repay, says the Lord." (Romans 12:19)*

The justice within the world is limited, not so with God; he is the righteous judge with power, authority and justice. Yet, he is so patient and loves us so much.

> *The LORD passed before him and proclaimed, "The LORD, the LORD, a God merciful and gracious, slow to anger, and abounding in steadfast love and faithfulness, keeping steadfast love for thousands, forgiving iniquity and transgression and sin, but who will by no means clear the guilty." (Exodus 34:6-7a)*

God brings perfect justice and His perfection when He comes back. Our part is to forgive our sins and others, and by his strength, we are empowered to do so because of the grace.

> *In this is love, not that we have loved God but that he loved us and sent his Son to be the propitiation [satisfaction] for our sins. (1 John 4:10)*

Do not be too hard on yourself in forgiving others! If you drop the charges against those who wronged you, you forgave them. When forgiving seems too hard to handle, God gives us His strength. Be free and give the offenses to God's capable hands. Jesus is constantly at work, advocating on behalf of His sheep with a plan of restoration and healing.

> *Be kind to one another, tenderhearted, forgiving one another, as God in Christ forgave you. (Ephesians 4:32)*

The picture of sheep pausing long enough to actually lie down on green pasture shows that sheep are fully satisfied. They are content. The second verse, "He makes me lie down in green pastures" is the result of the first verse, "The Lord is my shepherd. I shall not want."

John Goldingay described the picture in verse 2:

It implies that they have eaten, are satisfied, and have no need to move on to look for further grass: this pasture will provide the next meal, too. Lying down after feeding also hints at security (Ezekiel. 34:14-15; Zeph. 3:13, also Job 11:19; Isa. 17:2).[14]

The green pasture in Psalm 23:2 is a wonderful place where sheep can be fed with truth in a safe environment. Where the sheep can enjoy their meal in peace. One of the best places grow in truth is within a healthy church community who are led by wise shepherds. Pastors, leaders and elders of a church are often referred to as shepherds because they are to serve the people God brings (1 Timothy 3). When the leaders are deeply rooted in the word of God, then they are better equipped to love and serve their flock.

An interesting observation about the progression of the chapter is that the sheep go through the valley of the shadow of death (Chapter 6) *after* he or she is restored with food and the still water. Often, we may go through a dark place in our life after we experience the enrichment in our spirit. It is an indication of restored sheep.

I have said these things to you, that in me you may have peace. In the world you will have tribulation. But take heart; I have overcome the world." (John 16:33)

Despite all that, when we follow Jesus, we can be satisfied and secure in Him because He is our Good Shepherd, and because our identity is found in Christ.

꧁꧂

Jehovah-Shalom, God who gives peace

---

[14] Goldingay, John. Psalms: Psalms 1-41. United States of America, n.p, 2006.

Psalm 23:2a Discussion

- What stood out to you the most throughout this chapter?

- How important is it to study the Bible in context? What does this look like?

- What kind of impact does a Bible study have on spiritual health?

- What ways are there to study the Bible? What tools would enrich your time with God?

- Assess yourself: are properly being fed with the Word of God?

- Do you still feel hunger in your life? If you do, then search your heart and see what is missing in your life? Is Jesus satisfying you?

Chapter 4. Restoration by Still Water

"He leads me beside still water. He restores my soul"
Psalm 23:2b-3a

Scripture for deeper study: Psalm 51:1-17

৪১০৪৪

We experience different aspects of life and go through different stages in our thinking, processing and responding. These seasons are expanded upon in the first part of Ecclesiastes 3. Verse 1 emphasizes *for everything there is a season, and a time for every matter under heaven.* We each go through different seasons, difficult seasons, fun seasons, crazy seasons, seasons of trials and even seasons of healing when we surrender our hurts and the hurts done against us into the capable healing hands of Jehovah Rapha – The Lord Your Healer. We cannot control when each season comes our way, but we can control how we respond to it and allow God to be our anchor and restorer.

In our culture, we are often living as if we are running on a hamster wheel. We do not know where we are coming from or where we are going. Another example can be found in musical chairs: when the music starts, everyone moves around frantically until the music stops. While the people are running around the chairs with the music, the anxiety of losing a chair intensifies. People run around all over the place until they may become ill. Sheep need to rest from time to time.

Sheep are timid creatures that tend to follow without thinking. They need to be led to water that is quiet and easy to drink. If a sheep is lead to strong waters that are gushing all about, they may not process the dangers, get confused and easily topple into or be swept away by the rapids. Calm and still waters are very important for thirsty sheep to drink.

Part I. God is Steadfast

*E*ach one of us has a life story that God is weaving together. With each life testimony, we gain a broader view and understanding of the nature of God and our relationship with Him. Our lives are filled with all kinds of emotions, challenges and moments that build and define our character. Everyone experiences different kinds of difficulties, pain and suffering in life. Most of us are seeking to be healed from the pain and suffering that life brings us.

With great effort we seek happiness, but often we find that our aspirations fall short of fulfilling our hearts, leaving us running on empty. The unfulfillment sometimes leaves us disappointed, hurt or angry. If examined, our pain reveals truth and new understandings about life, God's love and healing. We then can empathize with others as well as share truth about God's steadfast love.

Sometimes, our pain allows us to be mature in understanding others at a deeper level instead of being self-centered. We learn to visit others with a sincerer heart and open our mouths carefully and wisely. We learn to be more sensitive to someone else's pain and sorrow. We do not allow the people in our life to getaway with the generic answer of, "I am fine" when asked "How are you?"

"All will be well" written by Dr. John DelHousaye.

> *Jacob offers one of the clearest exhortations to reframing in the New Testament. The verb to consider (hēgeomai) describes constrained thought. Obviously, our bent is not to find joy in suffering unless it is purposeful. A woman— so I am told—can suffer in labor as long as she knows the pain is temporary and culminates in the birth of her precious child (John 16:21). In the same way, a believer, through prayer and meditation on the Word of God, is able to reframe tragedy. Joy is not so much a feeling as*

an awareness of ultimate well-being: all is well because all will be well."[15]

Often, we meet Christians who have endured tremendous pain in their lives, yet they share their testimony with such reassurance, encouragement and hope. Like Job in the Old Testament who went through every devastation this world has to offer, he still took on a heart attitude of blessing God instead of blaming Him. Our hope comes from Romans 8:28, *"And we know that for those who love God all things work together for good, for those who are called according to his purpose."* Everyone has trouble, trials and pain while living in this broken world, but this is only temporary. As Christians, we have a hope and joy that extends beyond life on earth, into eternity in Heaven where God has fully expelled all evil from our lives, where tears and suffering have no power. That is why Christians repeatedly chose joy and confidence even when experiencing pain and suffering.

Throughout the restoration process, we experience the spiritual realm with an incomparable peace, love, and confidence, that only is experienced with our trusting and leaning on our heavenly shepherd.

We enter the Kingdom of God.

As we study Psalm 23, we realize, not just knowing or believing, but "awakening" to the truth that God is our Shepherd. Allowing God to reveal aspects of his nature that we may have ONCE only understood in our mind, but after going through a rough experience, we rely on Jehovah Jireh – God who provides, and now KNOW our heavenly shepherd with deeper understanding. This transitions our head knowledge into heart-experiential knowledge.

As we think of it, it is an astonishing and powerful truth when we trust and allow the personal, intimate and caring God to transform our hearts

---

[15] DelHousaye, John General Epistle and Revelation

40

and minds, we understand more deeply of the depths of his eternal love for us.

According to the book <u>Kingdom Priest</u>, by Eugene H. Merrill, in ancient times, there was a king named "Hyksos"; the name means "shepherd kings" in their context of ruler of the people.[16]

As we may have learned in World History, many generations of kings were brutal and violent towards their people to control them through a regime of power and fear or because they were greedy and did not care about the people. Kings may be threatened or frightened by adversaries trying to overthrow the king and take possession of the kingdom. It is more difficult to find a good, kind or generous king who was loved by his people. As the saying goes – whatever you own, owns you. For a king who has much is at greater risk to allow his possessions and power to dictate his actions, which may not always be in the best interests of the people.

However, our Shepherd is a kind shepherd who rescues us from the enemies of our soul. God is seated on the unshakable throne which no enemy or adversary can take away; His Kingdom is eternal, indestructible, and forever loving. His steadfastness manifests in love and kindness toward His people.

God is strong, secure and still, we can be as well when we choose to follow Him, allow Him to raise us into maturity and rest in this promise of God. What a blessing to follow the Shepherd who is kind and gentle, yet still, immovable. Sometimes we think gentle means someone who lacks strength, but in truth, gentle refers to intentionally withholding great strength on another's behalf. Our God is patient and gentle with us, yearning for us to come to him!

As mentioned earlier, sheep cannot and will not drink water from rapidly running water. In fact, they may often get swept away by the

---

[16] Merrill, Eugene H. (2008) Kingdom of priests: a history of Old Testament Israel. Grand Rapids, MI, Baker Academic.

rapids. Here is an example of watering sheep in ancient Israel. In Genesis 29:1-3,7-8,

> *Then Jacob went on his journey and came to the land of the people of the east. As he looked, he saw a well in the field, and behold, three flocks of sheep lying beside it, for out of that well the flocks were watered. The stone on the well's mouth was large, and when all the flocks were gathered there, the shepherds would roll the stone from the mouth of the well and water the sheep, and put the stone back in its place over the mouth of the well.*
>
> *He said, "Behold, it is still high day; it is not time for the livestock to be gathered together. Water the sheep and go, pasture them." But they said, "We cannot until all the flocks are gathered together and the stone* is rolled from the mouth of the well; then we water the sheep."

The shepherds waited until all the sheep were present and calm to provide them with safe water to drink.

> I want to share Dr. McGee's words. In his book, Psalms, *"Sheep are frightened by turbulent water. And they don't like stagnant water. They don't want to drink where the hogs drink. All of this applies to the human family."*[17]

God himself is our resting place, He is immovable. He is like this "Still water." We can drink His water! Look at John 4 to witness the Samaritan woman's experience with Jesus' living water.

Psalm 46 is a blessing to those who are weary. See the contrast of the powerful waters and how the Almighty God uses this picture of his strength, glory and peace that we may be still and trust God to restore us.

---

[17] McGee, J.Vernon. Psalms: Chapters 1-42. Nashville, Nelson, 1991.

God is our refuge and strength, a very present help in trouble.

Therefore we will not fear though the earth gives way, though the mountains be moved into the heart of the sea, though its waters roar and foam, though the mountains tremble at its swelling. Selah

There is a river whose streams make glad the city of God, the holy habitation of the Most High.

God is in the midst of her; she shall not be moved; God will help her when morning dawns.
The nations rage, the kingdoms totter; he utters his voice, the earth melts.

The LORD of hosts is with us; the God of Jacob is our fortress. Selah

Come, behold the works of the LORD, how he has brought desolations on the earth. He makes wars cease to the end of the earth; he breaks the bow and shatters the spear; he burns the chariots with fire.
"Be still, and know that I am God. I will be exalted among the nations, I will be exalted in the earth!"

The LORD of hosts is with us; the God of Jacob is our fortress. Selah

Many of us who have experienced an abortion or trauma might experience restlessness from shock, guilt and shame, maybe anger if there was an injustice or numbness if the pain has been buried and festering beneath the surface of our hearts.

When I lean on God who is "our resting place" I experience peace whenever that restless fear rears its demanding head.

Have you seen how a grapevine branch is anchored in Jesus' illustration of resting in John 15:4? Let's take a peek at it:

> *"Abide in Me, and I in you. As the branch cannot bear fruit of itself unless it abides in the vine, so neither can you unless you abide in Me."*

In this analogy, Jesus is the vine and we are the branches. Jesus is the logos, *words*, abide in his words and we can experience "**still water**" and plentiful food in green pastures.

On the way to the radio station, I saw a van with a sign which said, *"Healing the land, Going back to nature."* Lately, we hear messages about protecting nature or other environmental issues. In ancient Israel, Israelites intentionally rested their land, enabling the soil to regenerate nutrients, every seven years. They called that seventh year "Jubilee." They would not plant or harvest anything in that field. If our land needs rest and healing, how much more do humans need rest and healing? Of course, we talk about healing in the 21st Century, but I am not talking about a surface healing, but a deep inner healing of the soul. Let's look at the restoration process in connection with the word, "still".

How important it is for us as a society to be still by "the Still water" for healing. We know that a large population of our community is affected by abortion and devastating trauma and are in need of healing. As a whole, our society is in the midst of performing different rituals. They become chained to the cycle of seeking things to replace the pain, numb the hurt, or staying so busy we have no time to think, running to various idols, books, and help guides seeking for something to make it all better. Despite our efforts, the restlessness remains because we have not stopped to filter through our hurts.

Part II. Finding Rest & Restoration

$\mathcal{L}$et us see the restoration process in connection to the word "still."

We are going to look closer the word, "still".

> 4496. מְנוּחָה menuchah or מְנֻחָה menuchah (629d); fem. of
> 4494; resting place, rest: —comforting(1), permanent(1),
> place(1), place of rest(1), quartermaster*(1), quiet(1),
> rest(8), resting(1), resting place(7), resting places(1).

Psalm 46
> 7503. רָפָה raphah (951c); a prim. root; sink, relax:—
> abandon*(1), alone*(2), become helpless(1), become*(1),
> cease(2)

Genesis 2
> 7673a. שָׁבַת shabath (991d); a prim. root; to cease, desist,
> rest:—brought to an end.[18]

The root word, "still" in Psalm 23:3 is used in Genesis 8:4; and in the seventh month, on the seventeenth day of the month, the ark came to rest on the mountains of Ararat.

Can you imagine the storm that Noah's family had to go through? For forty days and nights of uncertainty in an ark surrounded by storms and darkness. We imagine how they lived daily without the sun. If they used any kind of lighting system, one simple mistake could burn the whole ark in a matter of time during the windy, powerful storm. Think of it, we see the hand of God in every detail.

---

[18] Thomas, R. L. (1998). New American Standard Hebrew-Aramaic and Greek dictionaries: updated edition. Anaheim: Foundation Publications, Inc.

Check out Genesis 8:4, after the heavy storm, as the ark rested on the mountains of Ararat, which means "the curse reversed; precipitation of a curse."[19]

As the ark was led to rest on the mountains of Ararat, the shepherd leads the sheep to still water to restore them. God is also leading you to the still water. Be still as God leads you to still water. Do not be frightened. God will give you rest and restore you.

There is a connection with the words, return, repent and restore in their Hebrew context; a unique language that expresses such spiritual depth within one word.

The definition of the word "shub" used for "restores" is described as follows:

שׁוּב shub (996d); a prim. root; to turn back, return: repent(6), repent and turn away(2), repentant(1), restitution which is made(1), restore(58), restored(17), restorer(2), restores(7), restoring(1), restrain(2, retire(1), return(261), return and take back(1).[20]

There is often a muddled sense of being lost after returning home from a long journey; we need to process, reflect, or assess where we were before and after the journeyed experiences and the impact of those experiences with our future steps. When life experiences take a path of turmoil, our faith and trust in our shepherd is questioned, will we lean on Him or our own human reasoning? Will there be still water or restless fear? If the latter, we know we can return to the Shepherd and choose to stay with Him

Each generation releases a different zeal in sharing the truth of God, but recent generations' passion often adds shame and guilt to change peoples' hearts to the Shepherd. For some, the harshness penetrates

---

[19] Dr. Judson Cornwall & Dr. Stelman Smith, The Exhaustive Dictionary Of Bible Names
[20] Thomas, R. L. (1998). New American Standard Hebrew-Aramaic and Greek dictionaries: updated edition. Anaheim: Foundation Publications, Inc.

their thickly-walled heart, but for others, it only creates thicker walls. We want to help our fellow sheep get past the accusations and offenses of being sinners to accepting the loving and just truths of the Shepherd and giving our hearts to sweet surrender and the beautiful repentance. According to Dr. John DelHousaye (p.126) in his writing General Epistles and Revelation.

> *We should also confess our sin to those we have personally wronged. Confession heals strained relationships…So confession is a regular part of our marriage. Tiffany and I find ourselves in that difficult yet realistic tension of understanding but not enabling our sins toward one another. Love should be unconditional, but also hopeful.*[21]

Verse 4 talks about the righteousness after restoration. We understand our wrongdoings because God gave us the law as a reflection of who He is and how we were designed to live.

> [23] *Now before faith came, we were held captive under the law, imprisoned until the coming faith would be revealed.* [24] *So then, the law was our guardian until Christ came, in order that we might be justified by faith.* [25] *But now that faith has come, we are no longer under a guardian,* [26] *for in Christ Jesus you are all sons of God, through faith. (Galatians 3:23-26)*

When we reject God's design, life becomes extra complicated, but when we confess our failure to align ourselves with God, and accept the truths that God wants to give us, then we grant God permission to transform that area of our life. We then transition from being under the law to being under faith – which is simply believing God. Walking by faith is what God counts as righteousness. When we try to be righteous by the things we do, that is self-righteousness and prevents God's healing from penetrating into the deepest areas of our heart and soul.

---

[21] DelHousaye, John General Epistle and Revelation

⁹ If we confess our sins, he is faithful and just to forgive us our sins and to cleanse us from all unrighteousness. ¹⁰ If we say we have not sinned, we make him a liar, and his word is not in us. (1 John 9-10)

ഇൗ രൂ

Jehovah-Rophe, God who heals

Psalm 23:2b-3a Discussion

- What stood out to you the most throughout this chapter?

- With our busy schedules, how important is it for us to stop and rest our heart and mind to walk through healing? How do we do this?

- What would finding rest look like for you this week?

- How do you perceive the still water in Psalm 23:3?

- What does "Be Still" mean?

- What is one of God's attributes or characteristics that we can cling too as we seek rest and restoration by still water.

Chapter 5. Paths of Righteousness

"He leads me in paths of righteousness
for His name's sake"
Psalm 23:3b

Scripture for deeper study: Psalm 51:1-17

ഇരു

*F*aith begins, rests and ends in Christ.[22]

We are justified before God in Christ alone.
We are sanctified in Christ alone through the Holy Spirit.
We are going to be glorified in Christ alone.

Part I. Paths

*A*s the saying goes, life is a marathon, not a sprint. Some of us try to rush ahead, going full speed and then we get burned out, exhausted and discouraged when things do not go the way we planned. Other times, we try to go on our own wandering path, which brings us with thistles, branches and thorny cacti that require extra detours, slow us down and leave wounds and scars. The path that leads to life and righteousness is narrow and not without its challenges, but it is a path that refines our character and leads us in the direction that God desires.

We are made righteous through the blood of Jesus. He is our High Priest and when God looks upon us, He sees Jesus' blood and sacrifice so that we can stand before God without condemnation. How Wondrous! How comforting that we can place our faith and trust in a dependable God. We are not righteous by our own merit; no amount of good deeds will make us righteous.

---

[22] M Charles Bell, Calvin and Scottish Theology, Doctrine of Assurance P 19-21.

Part II. Righteousness

We are going to study the word, "righteousness" in this chapter.

How many people are struggling from self- righteousness? I struggle a lot.

Galatians 6:1 explains how to face struggles.

> *Brothers, if anyone is caught in any transgression, you who are spiritual should restore him in a spirit of gentleness. Keep watch on yourself, lest you too be tempted. (Galatians 6:1)*

Also, James 5:13-20 gives us instruction about praying for others and the responsibility to acknowledge our sins too.

The Prayer of Faith

> *Is anyone among you suffering? Let him pray. Is anyone cheerful? Let him sing praise. Is anyone among you sick? Let him call for the elders of the church, and let them pray over him, anointing him with oil in the name of the Lord. And the prayer of faith will save the one who is sick, and the Lord will raise him up. And if he has committed sins, he will be forgiven. Therefore, confess your sins to one another and pray for one another, that you may be healed. The prayer of a righteous person has great power as it is working. Elijah was a man with a nature like ours, and he prayed fervently that it might not rain, and for three years and six months it did not rain on the earth. Then he prayed again, and heaven gave rain, and the earth bore its fruit.*
>
> *My brothers, if anyone among you wanders from the truth and someone brings him back, let him know that whoever brings back a sinner from his wandering will*

save his soul from death and will cover a multitude of sins.

As James 5:19-20 explains, how important it is to look out for the people around us. Jesus is in the business of saving the unrighteous.

An interesting finding is that the word, "righteousness" when written in Chinese uses the characters of lamb on the top of "I (ego) or Me" in English. I do not know how the word was formed, what kind cultural background, but it is interesting how they communicated the word, "righteousness" in China. Something interesting to research: how the Chinese form their pictorial language.

It is impossible for humans to be righteous of our own accord. As we get older, we realize more and more something is wrong with us. We try to be perfect in so many ways, yet soon we become exhausted from trying harder and harder. We become restless. The Chinese character for the word, "righteousness:"

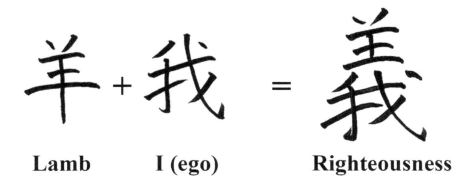

Lamb   I (ego)   Righteousness

The "lamb" is above "I"; the Lamb of God is our righteousness. What is so amazing about this picture is how Jesus was referred to as the Lamb of God.

> *The next day he saw Jesus coming toward him, and said, "Behold, the Lamb of God, who takes away the sin of the world! (John 1:29)*

The *Lamb of God* is the title given to Jesus who came as the perfect sacrifice to pay for our wrongdoings and unrighteousness. This is one of the heaviest and most meaningful titles as we stand back in awe of the weight of this great sacrifice that was paid.

In the Old Testament, the Israelites practiced animal sacrifices to God that served as a picture of Jesus who was to come. When God rescued the Israelites from slavery in the land of Egypt, under the reign of Pharaoh (Exodus 12), God had each household sacrifice a lamb without blemish, and put some of the blood on their door posts.

> *The blood shall be a sign for you, on the houses where you are. And when I see the blood, I will pass over you, and no plague will befall you to destroy you, when I strike the land of Egypt. (Exodus 12:13)*

The blood of the sacrificial lamb protected the people from the destroyer. In the same way, Jesus is the perfect sacrificial lamb without blemish. Jesus died on the cross at the exact time when the Passover lamb was sacrificed in the temple. Jesus is the Lamb of God who came back to life according to the prophecies. When God looks at us who have chosen to be children of God, Jesus' blood is what God now sees and his judgement passes over us. The righteousness of God is then shared with us who believe in Jesus by Faith and He gives us a promise to look forward too:

> *For the Lamb in the midst of the throne will be their shepherd, and he will guide them to springs of living water, and God will wipe away every tear from their eyes. (Revelation 7:17)*

As we abide in Jesus, we experience the life of righteousness that He shares with us, which is not possible without Jesus; the Lord gives us the strength to follow Him, His Righteousness.

"Sanctification" is the process we go through to be more like our Shepherd. The trials of become less formidable when pursuing God as He gently works, exposing areas in our life that he wants to work on, each in its season. As we agree with God that we want to allow Him to work in an area, then God continues to mold and shape us more into His likeness. This ongoing process is what we call sanctification. As a result, we seek more of Jesus; we then can rest as we allow the Shepherd Lord to guide us rather than exhausting ourselves by donning our own righteousness. We can rest when we stop trying our way.

Part III. Whose sake?

We are living in a time when every health issue seems to be resolved by taking medicine. Of course, medicine is one of the greatest inventions and has advanced tremendously to improve health and well-being through procedures and medicine. However, the misuse or over dependence on medicine can sometimes cause more harm than healing. In the early days of medicine, the doctor would look at the patient as a whole person, yet did not have full understanding of the particulars of the different systems within the human body, but used the overall condition to determine a course of healing,

In present day, our medical field emphasizes specializations of each individual system that the unity of a person's body, heart, mind and soul has nearly been lost. Yet because of the pendulum of extremes, holistic and homeopathic medicine is gaining ground because it is so intentional to look for ways to help your body heal itself, while recognizing the interconnectedness of all of the bodily systems.

The Good Shepherd is also called the Great Physician and He is the ultimate healer, addressing our physical, emotional and mental needs by transforming the spiritual. We too, can get so distracted by a specific system that we are dealing with, that we miss the big picture of why it needs to be addressed.

And when Jesus heard it, he said to them, "Those who are
well have no need of a physician, but those who are sick. I
came not to call the righteous, but sinners." (Mark 12:17)

If our heart is having issues, we may need to go on a heart monitor, but we know that our doctor is keeping an eye on everything that is happening and has the qualification and skills to prescribe a treatment. In the same way, God is constantly working in our lives, shaping and molding us more and more into his likeness – the process of sanctification. And although the cleaning up process may hurt, and we cannot understand why something is happening, we know that the Great Physician is qualified and skilled at the work He is doing in our lives.

We each have our own life to live. No two lives are identical. This also means that our journeys are different and although we may all be traveling upon this narrow path, our adventures on it may look a little different. To one person, God has given an extra passion for evangelism, to another, a heart of service, still another, a love of helping children grow into maturity. As we each utilize the gifts and passions that God has given us, then we can better serve one another in love until Jesus' return.

When taking on the role of a shepherd, taking the time to know and understand the sheep from a holistic perspective will enable us to meet the sheep where they are at and help them get to where they want to be. To diagnose patients accurately, a doctor needs to fully watch and listen to the patient, looking at their symptoms, verbal explanations and body language. When we listen hastily, or make assumptions, we are at risk for missing an important piece of the puzzle in the journey of healing.

> *"The broadest word for health in the Bible is shalom,*
> *"peace." It encompasses physical, mental, ecological, social,*
> *and spiritual well-being. Confession is the maintenance of*
> *shalom with God. Sin attacks shalom. When Christians*
> *sin, this displeases God and hurts the immediacy of the*
> *relationship. I do not believe we lose our standing before*

God every time we sin, because that standing is secured by our Lord and Savior, Jesus Christ. But any honest disciple will acknowledge that our relationship with God is like a marriage: un-confessed sin breaks down communication and the relationship becomes distant. The claim that confession is no longer necessary for Christians is unbiblical. James is not addressing Pagans but believers, and is not offering a suggestion, but a command. The Lord's Prayer assumes confession, at least to God, is a daily practice, like eating.[23]"

When our Shalom is restored, we experience a sense of right. As we mature in Shalom, we experience the Lord is guiding us to His Righteousness.

Faith begins, rests and ends in Christ alone.[24]
Again,

We are justified before God in Christ alone.
We are sanctified in Christ alone through the Holy Spirit.
We are going to be glorified in Christ alone.

☙❧

Jehovah-Tzid'Ke-nu, God is the righteous one, our righteousness

---

[23] DelHousaye, John General Epistle and Revelation
[24] M Charles Bell, Calvin and Scottish Theology, Doctrine of Assurance p19-21.

Psalm 23:3b Discussion

- What stood out to you the most about this chapter?

- What relationship does repentance have with restoration?

- What is repentance?

- What relationship does restitution and reconciliation have with restoration?

- What is the end result when we are restored by God?

- What does peace look like? How can you live out Shalom this week?

- Describe in your own words what does it look like if "Faith begins, rests and ends in Christ?"

- What is the path way of righteousness?

Chapter 6. You Are With Me

*"Even though I walk through the valley of the shadow
of death, I will fear no evil, for you are with me."*
Psalm 23:4a

Scripture for deeper study: Psalm 139:1-18
ℰℛ

𝒥n relationships, we know that our closest friends are on our side. They are rooting for us and we trust them. When we face difficulties, the challenges can be easier to bear. Depending on who is with us, the matters we "fear" can magnify in our life or lose its power.

Throughout life, we experience great times that we associate with being on a mountain top, like being on top of the world. On the other side, life can be hard, and our lowest times can be associated with deep valleys. David has been through valleys, darkness and death. These valleys may include his many enemies, those who have wronged him, and even those he has wronged, like his friend Uriah the Hittite who he had killed, Bathsheba and their first baby who died. We may be surprised at the depth of our emotions, when we see or feel an injustice and the wrongs done towards ourselves or others.

In Psalm 23:4, David is reflecting on past circumstances where death was lurking, but instead of letting the shadow overtake him, David looks straight forward resolutely, denying the fear that tries to have power over him. No matter what David faced, sometimes he was successful, and other times he failed miserably, regardless, he continually sought to make himself right before God. Even when our circumstances seem greater than we can handle or process, we can trust God, our Shepherd is with us and we can trust Him.

David did not write "you are with me" on other verses like when sheep was in green pastures, still water or path of righteousness, etc, but rather on the verse 4 while he was taking about the valley of shadow of death. We experience strong intimacy with God while we go through the dark times.

Part I. In the Valleys

When we experience the valley of the shadow of death, we can also experience the unshakable "Shalom" or peace that comes from resting in the presence of God. Even if we are in a difficult situation, in our spirit, we can be like a sparrow who is free from fear because the Lord is with us, just as David confessed in Psalm 23:4; *for you are with me.*

God allows us to go through these low places, perhaps the loss of loved one, chronic illness, financial, accident or any kind of hardship. We cannot deny something is wrong in our place that we call earth.

When we are in so much pain that seems like no one can comfort us, we need to watch how God provides a resource or person who experienced or understands the pain and shares comfort with us. Sometimes we want to just have someone near us who understands and other times we seek someone who listens us. We become comforted as though we are sitting with Jesus; the beauty of ministering is comforting others with the heart of Jesus. Remember too, those who experienced abortion often suffer silently and also need compassion, especially by those of us who already experienced healing from its confusing emotional and sometimes physical pains.

Often our cultural influences use shame and guilt in punishment for a "wrongdoing," I would like to share with our readers about the book that I just ordered. The renowned international Christian apologist Ravi Zacharias' testimony was also briefly mentioned. Ravi had attempted suicide at one point when he was younger, but was not motivated by depression, instead it was because of the cultural shame due to his poor grade performance. The title is <u>Ministering in Honor – Shame Cultures</u> by Jayson Gregory and Mark D. Backer.

> *"A foreign culture is like the night sky-initially fascinating, but quickly daunting without configuration to meaningfully connect the dots. Amateur stargazers see stars; but missed the constellations. Honor-shame is like the lines between stars; they give meaning and structure to life. Westerners rarely get honor-shame dynamic; they seem foreign. When we fail to disconnect the dots, we experience cultural frustration and miss kingdom opportunities. In light of the prominence of honor and shame for shaping life in many cultures, too much is at stake to not account for them in Christian mission."*[25]

I encountered numerous people who experienced abortion. Christ came to save those who live under shame, guilt and illness in their inner being, not to shame them.

When I step out to the public to share hope and encouragement in our ministry, I had to overcome the social messages that put me in more dangerous place than an actual abortion; that is honor and shame issue; I stepped out boldly. Some might have thought that I was foolish. I was born in a third-generation Christian family from my mother side, my grand uncle was a congress man and heavily involved in politics. Our family was raised in a culture with extreme measures for honor and shame. I ran all my life to build honor by pursuing education, supporting my husband's success and raising my children to live an honorable life. What I do in my later years of my life was not something I had planned out. However, I will not trade my passion with anything at my age. I still believe the importance of having a voice for unborn children and their parents, who are living under shame and guilt, reinforced by our media and political portrayals of abortion; for me, it will never be a superfluous

---

[25] Georges, J., & Baker, M. D. (2016). Ministering in honor-shame cultures: Biblical foundations and practical essentials. Downers Grove, IL: IVP Academic.

issue. I step out to share my story to comfort others and foster a healthy perspective rather than oppression for their journey of healing.

Walking with people who are suffering helps them carry their heavy load when you lend your time, quiet strength, gentle courage and continuous prayer. As I witness people released from their suffering, I remember God's provision and I can be faithful to God and stay in God's calling. I could not quit because I do know there are numerous people still suffering from abortion and I believe in healing. The real strength is coming from God when He heals our inner being.

We come back into Our Good Shepherd's arms and weep. It is okay. When we experience God's love, we experience our strength is coming back as we are empowered by the power of the Holy Spirit.

We can experience "You are with me." When we come to church on Sunday, God is waiting for us with open arms, with his beloved people all gathered together in one sweet community. Also understand everyone in the church is vulnerable like many of us, including leaders. We come to the church to meet our Heavenly Father and our fellow sheep. Be encouraged by Psalm 84:1-7.

> *How lovely is your dwelling place,*
> *O Lord of hosts!*
> *My soul longs, yes, faints*
> *for the courts of the Lord;*
> *my heart and flesh sing for joy*
> *to the living God.*
> *Even the sparrow finds a home,*
> *and the swallow a nest for herself,*
> *where she may lay her young,*
> *at your altars, O Lord of hosts,*
> *my King and my God.*
> *Blessed are those who dwell in your house,*
> *ever singing your praise! Selah*
> *Blessed are those whose strength is in you,*

in whose heart are the highways to Zion.
As they go through the Valley of Baca
they make it a place of springs;
the early rain also covers it with pools.
They go from strength to strength;
each one appears before God in Zion.

The valley of Baca is the valley of Mourning or Weeping. As a nation, Israel went through numerous hardship and oppression as we know. They had to depend on God who had chosen and called them.

Part II. Good times & Bad times

*W*hen things are going well, we may be tempted to feel self-sufficient or independent, presuming that all is well with the world. Watch out! Pride is lurking and often catches us off guard if we are not careful. This is our time to listen to the Shepherd's voice without distraction, following in his footsteps, soaking up the sun, rolling in the grass, drinking delicious clean water, meditating on God's word and spending sweet time with Him. Protect this restful time to renew and replenish your heart and soul.

For others of us, the good times are the easiest times to draw close to God because things are going so well that our fears are minimized to seem non-existent.

> *He has told you, O man, what is good; and what does the*
> *Lord require of you but to do justice, and to love kindness,*
> *and to walk humbly with your God? (Micah 6:8)*

Being a Christian does not guarantee the luscious green pastures and perfectly still water all the time with flowers blooming and the sun rays dancing with happiness strewn in every corner. There is often a valley of the shadow of the death looming overhead seeking to kill, steal and destroy the joys we have in Christ. We do not always experience deliverance from a bad situation, but God does promise to walk with us in the midst of the valley and hard times. Life can be messy sometimes, but through that pain and messiness, God is teaching us how to be more like himself. Regardless of the valleys, God is able to provide exactly what we need.

> *Fear not, for I am with you; be not dismayed, for I am your God; I will strengthen you, I will help you, I will uphold you with my righteous right hand. (Isaiah 41:10)*

When evil visits our life, seek God's direction, strength and even forgiveness. When we look at David's life, we can see his fearlessness when he faced the bears, lions and even Goliath, but when he himself was caught up in evil, this was a dark moment in his life which left him in a very vulnerable place.

Fear is a formidable enemy, but here is an opportunity to face those fears, confess our sins, like David confessed his sin before God with a contrite and remorseful heart, then God was given permission to work in the situation and David was able to resume his walk with God without sin hindering their relationship. Some of these fears may be magnified from the condemning messages present in some social campaigns involving abortion. Many of us who have experienced an abortion may be living under the oppression of fear.

> *I lift up my eyes to the hills. From where does my help come? My help comes from the Lord, who made heaven and earth. (Psalm 121:1-2)*

Do you feel that you are in a similar place as David?
Perhaps you are a CEO, lawyer, doctor, teacher, parent, manager, overseer, elder, pastor or in another type of leadership role who was in a position that provided strength and success. Maybe you have experienced that place in life where you feel like you are strong enough to conquer the world, and yet, a moment later, when you are by yourself, feel so weak and vulnerable? Even when we feel helpless and difficult to look inside, Jesus, your Shepherd is with you. Call on Him, He is mighty to sustain us and gives us to overcome the situation.

I know how to be brought low, and I know how to abound. In any and every circumstance, I have learned the secret of facing plenty and hunger, abundance and need. I can do all things through him who strengthens me. (Philippians 4:12-13)

As we shared earlier, those fears can be broken down, analyzed carefully and interpreted with the right filter. Identifying those fears, calling them out and replacing those lies with the Truth of God is very helpful in the healing process.

Fear and darkness come from the absence of God's truth and presence. God is everywhere, we call it "Omnipresence." However, in many cases, we isolate ourselves from the presence of God as Adam and Eve did. We believe lies such as, God is disappointed with us, we are worthless, not valuable, not a good Christian...etc. The enemy is on the prowl, wanting us to choose anything except God's reality and way of doing things. The truth is that we are a child of God (1 John 3:1-2) Christ's friend (John 15:15) New Creation (2 Corinthians 5:17); and He loves you with an everlasting love (Jeremiah 31:3).

So Jesus said to the Jews who had believed him, "If you abide in my word, you are truly my disciples, and you will know the truth, and the truth will set you free." (John 8:31-32)

These fears can be put to sleep when we experience "Shalom."

The opposite of fear is love. We can take our fears and replace it with God's love, promises, truth and experience "Shalom." When we trust God, we experience "Shalom."

When I was living in trauma and fear, Pastor Darryl DelHousaye preached about joy. He said that joy is absence of fear and suggested to memorize and recite Psalm 23.

There is no fear in love, but perfect love casts out fear. For fear has to do with punishment, and whoever fears has not been perfected in love. (1 John 4:18)

Fear	Truth	Verse
Fear of sin; fear of doing something wrong	God has forgiven us	1 John 1:9 Psalm 147:3
Fear of losing; aging; what has been given, also seems to be taken away	Eternal hope where we will not lose anything anymore	Psalms 30:10-11 Revelation 21:4
Fear from Trauma; scars	God's healing and restoration	Psalm 103:2-4
Fear of false guilt	Our sins are forgiven	Isaiah 43:25
Fear of damnation	There is no condemnation	Romans 8:1
Fear of God; fear that God is angry at us	God rejoices over us	Zephaniah 3:17
Fear of unknown	God is our Shepherd	Psalm 23:1

Phillip Keller in his book, A Shepherd Look at Psalm 23:

"The corollary to this is that only those who have been through such dark valleys can console, comfort or encourage others in similar situations. Often, we pray or sing the hymn requesting God to make us an inspiration to someone else. We want, instinctively, to be a channel of blessing to other lives. The simple fact is that just as water can only flow in a ditch or channel or valley—so in the Christian's career, the life of God can only flow in blessing through the valleys that have been carved and cut into our own lives by excruciating experiences.

For example, the one best able to comfort another in bereavement is the person who himself has lost a loved one. The one who can best minister to a broken heart is one who has known a broken heart."[26]

---

[26] Keller, W. Phillip. A Shepherd Looks at Psalm 23. Zondervan, 2015.

Part III. Together at ALL Times.

There is one kind of fear that we often shun and misconstrue as a spiritual condition; yet it is a condition of the mind. Oftentimes, when someone is experiencing severe anxiety or fear, spiritual weakness is not always the culprit, but may often be instigated from a tremendously traumatic experience. These experiences may cause extreme anxiety, fear or both and may even experience Post-Trauma Amnesia, memory loss around the traumatic experience.

Unfortunately, when a society is riddled with toxicity, the presence of abuse and trauma is ignored in so many lives. We have the opportunity to promote healing and healthy relationships, speaking truth and hope into some of the most abandoned areas of our lives. Like with any injury, if left untreated, the consequences can be detrimental as the trauma festers, tearing family and relationships apart.

The responsibility to seek help falls to us that are hurting and for others to be aware and step in and assist with the hurting burden—but we are to humble ourselves before God so that we can cast our cares on Him. Also, the verse that speaks to carrying one another's burdens—to walk alongside those hurting individuals, doesn't mean that others must take over and the hurt do nothing; even the patient awaiting surgery much come prepared.

We each respond to our hurts in different ways; some of us choose a flight response and run away into the innermost parts of our mind and imagination. Others of us may resonate with a physical response that may turn extremely violent. When we are wounded, we do not always process things clearly and when we feel like we are not being heard and understood, we may resort to hurting other people; maybe repeating behavior that was done to us.

Let's take a moment to think and process how you tend to respond. Is there a situation even in the last week where you had something that triggered your fears and you responded in a less than loving way?

According to Dr. Gary Smalley's <u>DNA of Relationships</u>, he expresses what he calls, the *Fear Dance*[27] which embodies the dangerous cycle that can occur when we have a fear, then respond in a certain way, which feeds into someone else's fear, who responds a certain way, which feeds back into my fear, and pretty soon we have an escalated fear dance that is spiraling out of control, leaving chaos and brokenness in its wake.

We believe God who is near to the brokenhearted and saves those who are crushed in spirit (Psalm 34:18). When we are in our lowest of lows, that is when God seems even closer in those moment; we are more focused in hearing God's voice. He can heal our brokenness, our emotions, our thinking, our body and our spirit. When it seems overwhelming, break it down into smaller pieces. These smaller pieces, our actions and attitudes, are symptoms that allow us to get to the root of the confusion and pain.

We are not alone in this process. In John 14 &15, Jesus encourages us by explaining how he sent us the Holy Spirit, who will be our helper and will be with us forever, he is the spirit of truth. Once we have identified our root issues, then we can assess which pieces are founded in truth and which pieces are founded in a lie. The Holy Spirit will also teach us the truth of God and help us to remember and recognize the truth from the lies. Once the lies have been isolated, then the lies need to be renounced and replaced with the Truth of God so that we can experience true freedom and deliverance.

Have you experienced one of those moments where it seems like time has completely stopped? One day, while I was in my backyard, my eyes caught the sight of a sparrow and time seemed to be frozen. I just stared at her for a long time. She seemed so oblivious and hopping on the green grass, so freely and without any fear. The joy of watching her in the moment was a sweet gift from God to me. Sometimes God wants us to live like this sparrow. Living in present moment is enjoying God's presence; God is with us in every circumstance.

---

[27] Smalley, G. (2007). *The DNA of relationships.* Wheaton, IL: Tyndale House. ISBN-13: 978-0842355322

This reminds me of a song that I learned when I was on a retreat during my college years in Korea. A missionary taught us this song in English.

"His Eye Is on the Sparrow" by Civilla D. Martin

Why should I feel discouraged,
why should the shadows come,
Why should my heart be lonely,
and long for heaven and home,
When Jesus is my portion? My constant friend is He:
His eye is on the sparrow, and I know He watches me;
His eye is on the sparrow, and I know He watches me.
Refrain:
I sing because I'm happy,
I sing because I'm free,
For His eye is on the sparrow,
And I know He watches me.

"Let not your heart be troubled," His tender word I hear,
And resting on His goodness, I lose my doubts and fears;
Though by the path He leadeth, but one step I may see;
His eye is on the sparrow, and I know He watches me;
His eye is on the sparrow, and I know He watches me.

Refrain

Whenever I am tempted, whenever clouds arise,
When songs give place to sighing, when hope within me
dies, I draw the closer to Him, from care He sets me free;
His eye is on the sparrow, and I know He watches me;
His eye is on the sparrow, and I know He watches me.[28]

---

[28] Morgan, R. J. (2003). Then sings my soul: 150 of the world's greatest hymn stories. Nashville, TN: Thomas Nelson.

Like the sparrow, we can freely hop around and bask in the presence of God without fear, because His eyes are on us, looking out for us, He is with us.

෪෬

Jehovah-Shammah, the Lord is there

Psalm 23:4a Discussion

- What stood out to you the most about this chapter?

- Describe a time in your life where you were walking through your own valley?

- How did you respond? How do you want to respond when future Valleys come?

- Do you experience "fear" in your life? Can you describe it?

- How do you tend to respond when your fears are triggered?

- How can you change your response the next time a fear comes?

- Describe the characteristics of the One who is with you? Who is with you?

- Why was a sparrow used to illustrate living with God without fear?

Chapter 7. Rod & Staff Comfort Me

"Your rod and Your staff, they comfort me."
Psalm 23:4b

Scripture for deeper study: Psalm 27:1-14
ಸಾ ೧೩

*W*hat is the rod and staff used for? The rod is a symbol of power and authority, the one who can bring about justice, leadership, rescuer and protector. The staff is an instrument of support and guidance.

For the early Israelites in slavery, the rod and staff of pharaoh signified his authority and rule over the nations. Pharaoh was renowned throughout the world as the mediator between the gods and man, a role passed on from father to son and their great prosperity was credited to their many gods. The rod and staff were symbols of the sovereign, their power reinforced through fear because one wrong move could result in death.

For those of us with a less than ideal example of a father or power figure in our lives, we may think of a strong hand or forceful submission to abuse, this is not the power we see in Psalm 23, instead we see the Good Shepherd.

Part I. Leader

*P*haraoh had a rod and staff, but Moses also had a staff. God freed his people Israel from Pharaoh's dominion, however, even though the Israelites were free in physical form from their 400 years as slaves in Egypt, their hearts and minds were still very much enraptured by the prosperity of Egypt. God took his people Israel led by Moses into the desert for 40 years to *cut out* the indulgent roots of the Egyptian culture along with the mindset of slavery out of the people. God then transformed the Israelite nation through their special time of resting with God in the desert in preparation to be a kingdom of priests to the world.

A priest is a person who is a mediator between God and man; someone who represented God like an ambassador. Moses was the man that God chose to represent himself to Israel, and Moses' brother Aaron, was the high priest who would make animal sacrifices to God on behalf of the Israelites. They were both responsible for relaying God's will, character and expectations to the people.

During their time in the desert, the people began to complain again and again about how life was better in Egypt. Egypt was known for having a surplus and spread of delicious food, fruits, bread and meat. In Numbers 11, the people remember the fish, cucumbers, melons, leeks, onions and garlic that they used to enjoy. Nevertheless, the people questioned why God brought them out into the seemingly barren desert, with no food or water and hope seemed to be lost. Moses, known as a friend of God, along with the people of Israel, had witnessed God's performance of several miracles in Egypt!

> *The Lord went ahead of them. He guided them during the day with a pillar of cloud, and he provided light at night with a pillar of fire. This allowed them to travel by day or by night. (Exodus 13:21 NLT)*

Exodus 7-15 details the miracles, plagues, the parting of the Red Sea, leading through the pillar of cloud and of fire and rescuing the whole nation of Israel; these were all great testimonies of God's provision, but the people continued to complain. Nevertheless, God had an awesome plan! The glorious presence of the Lord appeared, and then God commanded Moses:

> *Take the staff, and assemble the congregation, you and Aaron your brother, and tell the rock before their eyes to yield its water. So you shall bring water out of the rock for*

them and give drink to the congregation and their cattle."
(Numbers 20:8)

The staff – a symbol of leadership brings the people together to hear the word of the Lord. God was going to lead like a shepherd, that His people would know that God leads through his voice and that He is not like the Pharaoh who leads by the whip through fear and dominion, but by the authority from every word that comes from God and his compassionate heart. Sadly, Moses was so angry with the people, that he did not extend the holiness of God to the people.

Moses and Aaron, instead of speaking to the rock as God commanded, Moses insulted the people, grieved at their behavior and used the staff – a symbol of God's power, to hit the rock twice. God still brought the water to Israel, but the misuse of God's power did not reflect God's nature or desire to transform his people and required discipline of Moses. Moses did not get to enter the Promise Land (Numbers 20:6-12); Moses is a symbol of law. The event does signify that Moses did not go to heaven, rather signifies that no one can enter the heaven by law, but by grace alone.

Part II. Discipline – aka. training

*O*h discipline. For most of us, discipline is not a favorite word. However, in a proper Biblical context, this term brings greater understanding to the beautiful relationship we have with God. Discipline can also be described as training. Like how an athlete disciplines his body, while working towards a goal, eating healthy food, practicing his sport, and making the sacrifices to condition his body to be at its best. There may come a time where the coach may give a specific training regime to help the athlete grow beyond the original limits.

Remember how we learned that sheep are not the wisest creatures? When left on their own, they tend to lose their way. The shepherd must constantly talk to the sheep and even use goats and dogs to help train or discipline the sheep not to lose their way or fall into a ravine. I have a friend who used to raise sheep and she had to be very careful because if a little lamb was left alone, it would easily wander off, get into mischief or accidentally choke to death if it is left unattended.

The shepherd sees the big picture – he knows where the food and water are, he knows the terrain they travel on, he knows where the cliffs are or the dangerous places to avoid. He works hard to keep all the sheep on the right path. However, these precious sheep will often rebel, wander off or get themselves into trouble.

> *The Lord your God is in your midst, a mighty one who will save; he will rejoice over you with gladness; he will quiet you by his love; he will exult over you with loud singing. (Zephaniah 3:17)*

Because the Good Shepherd loves his sheep so much, when a sheep runs off too many times, getting into greater danger, the shepherd may break the legs of the sheep, to keep the sheep safe so that it will not wander off. But what is so beautiful is what happens after. The shepherd will not leave that sheep by itself in its misery and hurt, the shepherd will then pick up and carry that wandering sheep with broken legs and hold him so close so that the sheep will hear, listen and know the shepherd's voice. The Good Shepherd is so gentle, carrying the sheep everywhere he goes until the sheep's legs are fully healed. Their relationship will grow so tightly so that once the sheep's legs are healed, the sheep will never again wander off, not because of the loving chastening, but because of the sweet, loving relationship with the shepherd, because the sheep knows their shepherd.

As children of God, because he does not neglect us and is interested in our growth, our character development and our pursuit of righteousness, we have the privilege of receiving training and discipline. God's love for us is to refine and train us in the character of God during the trials and difficulties in our lives. It is easy to get caught up in the love and grace that we so heavily enjoy but forget the higher calling, moral standard and holy life that God commands us to pursue. Discipline should not be confused with the anger or wrath of God.

Our world has a lot of brokenness within our relationships and we do not always love and care for others as we should. <u>Abuse is not discipline</u>.

Think of a child who is playing in the kitchen and sees the handle of a pot of water boiling on the stove. As the child reaches to grab this new item, the parent may swoop in, whisk the child away, give a stern warning, a timeout, or redirect their small hands away from danger. The child may feel terrible, rejected, injustice, sad and even rebellious, but the loving parent knows that close guidance must be given to ensure the safety of that child from a serious burn. So as much as it pains them to enforce boundaries on the child, the parent only does so because they love the child so much and are looking out for their safety and well-being.

Hebrews 12:6-7a, 10-11 says following;

> *"For the Lord disciplines the one he loves, and chastises every son whom he receives." It is for discipline that you have to endure. God is treating you as sons... For they [earthly fathers] disciplined us for a short time as it seemed best to them, but he [God] disciplines us for our good, that we may share his holiness. For the moment all discipline seems painful rather than pleasant, but later it yields the peaceful fruit of righteousness to those who have been trained by it."*

If we think we have arrived at God's holiness or that we can achieve full completion while on this earth, then we are mistaken. We will never arrive at God's holiness on this side of heaven; there will always be room for Christ to continue transforming us, as he is preparing us for all eternity in heaven – a place grander and more wonderful than we can imagine. Evil will have no power or presence there. What a glorious day when we will be free from sin, shame and inadequacies, and live our true self as God meant us to be. We can rest in the peace, knowledge & joy that our God is Good with His infinite, enveloping, unconditional love. God will never forsake us, but on this earth, he promises to continue to teach and guide us, as we learn to trust and obey God in everything.

So be strong and courageous! Do not be afraid and do not panic before them. For the Lord your God will personally go ahead of you. He will neither fail you nor abandon you. (Deuteronomy 31:6 NLT)

Trials are not easy, but worth it!

Count it all joy, my brothers, when you meet trials of various kinds, for you know that the testing of your faith produces steadfastness. And let steadfastness have its full effect, that you may be perfect and complete, lacking in nothing. (James 1:2-4)

Part III. The Warrior, My Protector & Comforter

That night there were shepherds staying in the fields nearby, guarding their flocks of sheep. (Luke 2:8 NLT)

King David was a shepherd in his early years. During his time with the sheep, we read that he sang songs and made music in his quiet time while guarding his sheep. However, there were many enemies that went after his precious sheep. David fought off lions and bears and eliminated the threat. God protects his sheep.

There will be times when the enemy will come and attack; sometimes it will be the same enemy, and other times the threat looks different. The shepherd is always on guard for internal and external threats. So many things threaten the safety and prosperity of the sheep.

"Truly, truly, I say to you, he who does not enter the sheepfold by the door but climbs in by another way, that man is a thief and a robber. But he who enters by the door is the shepherd of the sheep. To him the gatekeeper opens. The sheep hear his voice, and he calls his own sheep by name and leads them out. When he has brought out all his own, he goes before them, and the sheep follow him,

for they know his voice. A stranger they will not follow,
but they will flee from him, for they do not know the voice
of strangers." This figure of speech Jesus used with them,
but they did not understand what he was saying to them.
So Jesus again said to them, "Truly, truly, I say to you, I
am the door of the sheep. (John 10:1-7)

The Good Shepherd protects and is with his sheep through every circumstance and threat. The close relationship that the sheep have was developed by listening and following the Shepherd's voice. A sheepfold is where the sheep will stay to rest for the night, and usually there is only one opening and the shepherd will stay with the sheep and sleep in that opening to protect the sheep throughout the night. The sheep are comforted by the Shepherd's presence and voice, knowing that he will protect them.

You go before me and follow me. You place your hand of
blessing on my head. (Psalm 139:5 NLT)

Our God fights for us, going before us, and following behind us, waging war on all our enemies. However, our enemies are very rarely in physical form. As Ephesians 6 emphasizes:

For we do not wrestle against flesh and blood, but against
the rulers, against the authorities, against the cosmic
powers over this present darkness, against the spiritual
forces of evil in the heavenly places. (Ephesians 6:12)

Our battle is not against flesh, but against the evil spiritual forces that are constantly warring for people's souls. We see this kind of battle played out throughout the Old Testament. Daniel had been praying, asking for God to make clear a vision he had seen. God had answered Daniel as soon as Daniel prayed and sent an angel to Daniel with the answer, but it took the angel three weeks to get the answer to Daniel.

And behold, a hand touched me and set me trembling on my hands and knees. And he [the angel messenger] said to me, "O Daniel, man greatly loved, understand the words that I speak to you, and stand upright, for now I have been sent to you." And when he had spoken this word to me, I stood up trembling. Then he said to me, "Fear not, Daniel, for from the first day that you set your heart to understand and humbled yourself before your God, your words have been heard, and I have come because of your words. The prince of the kingdom of Persia [fallen angel with authority] withstood me twenty-one days, but Michael [angel from God who protects Israel], one of the chief princes, came to help me, for I was left there with the kings of Persia [fallen angels], and came to make you understand what is to happen to your people in the latter days. For the vision is for days yet to come." (Daniel 10:10-14)

Daniel recognized the war that was present and persisted in his pursuit of God, trusting God in every circumstance. Another situation that plays out, representing God's mighty heavenly armies is seen in Elisha's story in 2 Kings. The king of Syria was mad that the prophet Elisha, kept getting in the way of his plans to conquer Israel so the king of Syria was determined to kill Elisha. He sent a great army with horses and chariots and surrounded the entire city where Elisha was staying. Elisha's servant woke up early and saw the enemy and was overwhelmed and reported immediately to Elisha who replied:

He [Elisha] said, "Do not be afraid, for those who are with us are more than those who are with them." Then Elisha prayed and said, "O Lord, please open his eyes that he may see." So the Lord opened the eyes of the young man, and he saw, and behold, the mountain was full of horses and chariots of fire all around Elisha. (2 Kings 6:16-17)

Elisha then asked God to blind the enemy and then the entire army was blinded, and Elisha lead the enemy army to the King of Israel in Samaria. Worth reading the whole story! God granted Elisha great victory over his enemies and the king of Syria stopped fighting against Israel.

When we are presented with a situation like Elisha's servant, coming across an enemy that seems to overwhelm us, we can respond like the servant or Elisha. Step back, remember the God we serve and that his Heavenly armies are much greater than those who are against us.

> Finally, be strong in the Lord and in the strength of his might. Put on the whole armor of God, that you may be able to stand against the schemes of the devil...Therefore take up the whole armor of God, that you may be able to withstand in the evil day, and having done all, to stand firm. (Ephesians 6:10-11, 13)

We have confidence in our Shepherd, who wields a rod and staff that represent God's full power and authority to lead, train, protect and fight for his sheep. God is good, fighting on our behalf against all the enemies we face in this world, seen and unseen. 1 Peter 5:8 compares our enemy as one who prowls like a roaring lion, seeking someone to devour. We serve a Good and Gracious God who is stronger than anything we come up against, he holds us close, drawing us closer to himself; as it says in 2 Chronicles 20:15, the battle belongs to the Lord. We walk in the Victory of the Lord because He has already won the war.

&⁓℞

Jehovah-Nissi, my banner, my refuge, who fights for me

Psalm 23:4b Discussion

- What stood out to you the most about this chapter?

- How did the Egyptians see the role of Pharaoh's "rod" and "staff"? How does God use these tools to show his character?

- How does a shepherd protect his sheep?

- In what ways has God been protecting and guiding you?

- What is the motivation for God's discipline?

- Why do we find comfort in the rod and staff?

- As part of the healing process, what areas of your life is God asking you to surrender to Him so that He can train you physically, emotionally, mentally and spiritually to help you grow stronger? (See Ephesians 6:10-18)

Chapter 8. More Than A Conqueror

"You prepare a table before me in the presence of my enemies."
Psalm 23:5a

Scripture for deeper study: 1 Peter 5:1-14
ॐ ଔ

𝒥 think that Psalm 23:5 is such an exciting verse! A wonderful table is prepared and laid out for us to replenish our strength, even though our enemies are all around. When I am overwhelmed by the pain and hurts inflicted by those whom I trusted, Psalm 23:5 brings about much hope and a different flavor in dealing with our enemies. In this chapter, we will dive a bit deeper into what it looks like to find peace, rest and nourishment in the midst of enemies.

We face many enemies, internal, external, physical or even our own memories or traumas may be a major enemy of our soul. Our response can look different depending on the enemy. Sometimes we need to forgive others, sometimes we need to forgive ourselves and other times, we need to stand our ground and persevere, fighting our enemies so that we are not chained by them.

> *"When you go out to war against your enemies, and see horses and chariots and an army larger than your own, you shall not be afraid of them, for the Lord your God is with you, who brought you up out of the land of Egypt. And when you draw near to the battle, the priest shall come forward and speak to the people and shall say to them, 'Hear, O Israel, today you are drawing near for battle against your enemies: let not your heart faint. Do not fear or panic or be in dread of them, for the Lord your God is he who goes with you to fight for you against your enemies, to give you the victory.' (Deuteronomy 20:1-4)*

I believe that we can arrive at that place where we can break the bread in the presence of our enemies, whatever they may look like, because we are trusting and dependent on the Good Shepherd who gives us victory. We also have the opportunity to break cycles in our own lives and prevent the brokenness from being passed down to future generations.

Part I. In the midst of chaos & brokenness

"*Table*" is "shulchan" in Hebrew. In Israel's early days, in the temple, God had the priests set up a table called the "Table of Presence [Shewbread]" which held fresh bread that always remained in the presence of God in the Holy place. Exodus 25:30$_{NKJV}$ affirms this with the command, *"And you shall set the showbread [shewbread, KJV] on the table before Me always."*

By design, the table and bread were an invitation to share a meal together, to show God's desire and willingness to have communion with mankind. The bread was then eaten by the priests, who represented God's people, on the Sabbath in the Holy place because the bread was Holy. Everything that God commanded in the Old Testament, presented a symbolic picture of the relationship that God desires to have with His people.

A relationship with you and with me! Jesus continues the symbolic illustration of bread.

> *This is the bread that comes down from heaven, so that one may eat of it and not die.* [51] *I am the living bread that came down from heaven. If anyone eats of this bread, he will live forever. And the bread that I will give for the life of the world is my flesh."* (John 6:50-51)

The bread in the temple was perishable, but through Jesus, he provides us with a bread (his very life, which is his words-logos) that is not perishable when we are in Him, our Good Shepherd.

We see a similar picture with communion—fellowship with God and his people. We can be united, be of one mind and one spirit because we are all one flock under the Good Shepherd.

> *Now as they were eating, Jesus took bread, and after blessing it broke it and gave it to the disciples, and said, "Take, eat; this is my body." (Matthew 26:26)*

Jesus is the life giver! Food is a universal language that we can all enjoy! God gives us rest and communion at His table, feeding us with His words of life. We may face difficulties, but God is big enough to take on anything that we may be facing. This is demonstrated so beautifully – even as the enemy or darkness seems to surround us, we can peacefully sit down at the Lord's table and enjoy fellowship with Him. The enemy has no power over us.

> *Again Jesus spoke to them, saying, "I am the light of the world. Whoever follows me will not walk in darkness, but will have the light of life." (John 8:12)*

We are identified by which side we choose. We choose the side of truth, living in the present reality that reflects the nature of God. We choose to agree with God that He has indeed set us free.

> *If you abide in my word, you are truly my disciples, and you will know the truth, and the truth will set you free." (John 8:31)*

If we are free, why then, is our struggle so real? We should be able to examine whether our choice is abided by the truth of God's reality, or bought into the lies, grudges and guilt of the enemy? We are to forgive, be at peace and love others with the Love that God showed us first, while we were still in sin as we see in 1 Corinthians 15:3 and Romans 5:8.

> *Bless those who persecute you; bless and do not curse them. (Romans 12:14)*

But I [Jesus] say to you, Love your enemies and pray for those who persecute you...For if you love those who love you, what reward do you have? (Matthew 5:44;46a)

*Since it is written, "You shall be holy, for I am holy."
(1 Peter 1:16)*

If possible, so far as it depends on you, live peaceably with all. Beloved, never avenge yourselves, but leave it to the wrath of God, for it is written, "Vengeance is mine, I will repay, says the Lord."

Do not be overcome by evil, but overcome evil with good. (Romans 12:18-19,21)

God knows us! He designed us! He even knows how to encourage us to endure so when things are rough, we may persevere through the difficulties.

When our enemies seem overpowering, we may feel discouraged, questioning our faith and wondering if God is still with us. God is absolutely with us in the midst of the darkness and is greater than all! He prepares a table before us in the midst of our enemies!

I am the Lord, and there is no other, besides me there is no God; I equip you, though you do not know me, that people may know, from the rising of the sun and from the west, that there is none besides me; I am the Lord, and there is no other. (Isaiah 45:5-6)

Also, Psalm 139:11-12

*If I say, "Surely the darkness shall cover me,
And the light about me be night,"
Even the darkness is not dark to you;*

The night is bright as the day,
for darkness is as light with you.

The darkness is not even dark to God. If we continue reading Psalm 139, we might become uncomfortable as I first did, having experienced an abortion. Although I love this poetic passage, for those of us whose brokenness or wounds are connected with an abortion, we want to take a careful approach when we share and study this passage and always with a motive of love.

There are wounds of the heart, although they are often concealed or hidden, that are still tender and vulnerable and require special care to heal properly. It can be so easy for us as Christians to use Bible verses to point out the specks of failure in everyone's life and forget the issues that we have dealt with in the past, are dealing with in the present or may need to address in the future. We each have different wounds to care for that are in different stages of healing.

As we went through tragic moments in our life, finding a trustworthy person, who walk alongside you in the journey of healing, can be vulnerable, yet so valuable process. We also want to offer grace to those who desire to help, even though they may go about it all wrong, lacking the finesse of addressing difficult issues! And through all things that we relate and communicate, may it be covered in prayer.

Psalm 139 also expresses the beauty of how God creates a baby in the womb! The process of having a baby is a unique and amazing experience. I remember how happy we were, especially my husband, Steven, when the baby was moving inside of me, it was the most mysterious and extraordinary joy that I have experienced. I am thankful that God allowed me the opportunity to still experience being a mother.

If you are at a dark place trying to navigate major life choices, rather than being scared and uncertain, we can be confident and trusting in our Creator God as we read a bit more of Psalm 139, allowing God to touch your soul, your identity and priceless value.

*You made all the delicate, inner parts of my body and knit
me together in my mother's womb.*

*Thank you for making me so wonderfully complex! Your
workmanship is marvelous—how well I know it.*

*You watched me as I was being formed in utter seclusion,
as I was woven together in the dark of the womb.*

*You saw me before I was born. Every day of my life was
recorded in your book. Every moment was laid out before
a single day had passed.*

*How precious are your thoughts about me, O God. They
cannot be numbered! I can't even count them; they
outnumber the grains of sand! And when I wake up,
you are still with me! (Psalm 139:13-18 NLT)*

Part II. Provision

Jehovah Jireh – the Lord will provide.

Remember Moses? The Egyptian prince turned Israelite fugitive, turned shepherd, turned God's messenger to Israel & the Egyptians. As friends speak with one another, so Moses conversed with God (Exodus 33:11). Through Moses, God freed the Israelites and then provided food from heaven, clothing that never wore out, water from rocks and protection from enemies. God provided for Moses and the Israelites as He led them with a pillar of cloud by day and pillar of fire by night.

Remember Abraham? Abraham called God—Jehovah Jireh! He was faced with the decision to trust God when he left his parents at age 75 and moved to the land God called him to, the land of Canaan. He trusted God's promise to provide a son in his old age. Abraham was then asked to give his only son Isaac, he trusted God to provide the sacrifice. As Abraham obeyed, God provided a ram for the offering (Genesis 22). Abraham was called a friend of God (James 2:23) and God counted Abraham's faith as righteousness in each situation.

Remember David? The king of Israel who was a very real person with victories, losses, challenges and strengths? God protected David from his enemies in so many ways so that David was successful in his reign; David was called a man after God's own heart (1 Samuel 13:14; Acts 13:22) and God was greatly glorified.

Remember Elijah? The prophet of God in the Old Testament who had the showdown on Mount Carmel. He challenged the Israelites by showing that God was real; God answered Elijah's sacrifice and prayer with a consuming fire from Heaven. Three years before that confrontation, there was a time when Elijah was utterly exhausted in 1 Kings 17, that he collapsed next to a brook Cherith, and then God ordered ravens to feed Elijah with bread and meat in the morning and evening. God literally provided food and water to Elijah! At the end of his life on earth, instead of dying, (2 Kings 2:11) God takes Elijah away in a chariot of fire!

Each of these men trusted God without knowing the end result! They believed God would provide what He promised. Hebrews 11 gives an astounding account of men and women who trusted, believed and obeyed God. Because of their faith, they grew closer in their relationship with God and God did some of the craziest and most awesome things imaginable!! This is the same God who loves you and desires to provide for you!

God provides a beautiful table of life, rest and peace in the midst of the distractions of chaos. We can confidently rest in the reality that God is the Creator of the universe and worthy of our praise! He is good, caring and comes alongside of us; we can trust Him because his promises are true, Elijah, David, Moses and others attest to these truths. Therefore, when the storms of life come, we will fear no evil, for God is with us! We are more than conquerors as we thrive in our relationship with God, enjoying the close conversation we have with God, our friend, the one whose heart we seek, the one who gives us new life.

Psalm 30:1-5 *Joy Comes with the Morning*
A Psalm of David. A song at the dedication of the temple.

*I will extol you, O Lord, for you have drawn me up and
have not let my foes rejoice over me*

*O Lord my God, I cried to you for help, and you have
healed me.*

*O Lord, you have brought up my soul from Sheol; you
restored me to life from among those who go down
to the pit.*

*Sing praises to the Lord, O you his saints, and give thanks
to his holy name.*

*For his anger is but for a moment, and his favor is for
a lifetime. Weeping may tarry for the night, but joy
comes with the morning.*

*in all these things we are more than conquerors through
him who loved us. (Romans 8:37)*

෨෬

Jehovah-Jireh, God will provide

Psalm 23:5a Discussion

- What stood out to you the most about this chapter?

- What did God do for David after he repented his sin? (2 Samuel 11-12)

- What would it look like in your life for God to prepare a table for you in the presence of your enemy?

- Who is Jehovah Jireh – the Lord will provide?

- Who is a person whom you look up to? What is it about them that inspires you?

- The Bible is full of regular men and women who believed and trusted God. Which hero of the faith do you resonate with the most? Why?

Chapter 9. Anointing

"You anoint my head with oil; my cup overflows."
Psalm 23:5b

Scripture for deeper study: Deuteronomy 20:1-4 & 1 Peter 5:1-14
ഇ൬

And without faith it is impossible to please him, for whoever would draw near to God must believe that he exists and that he rewards those who seek him. (Hebrews 11:6)

Anointing is an act that has roots with ancient shepherds. They would intentionally "anoint" the sheep by pouring oil over their head and face. Sheep are especially susceptible to bugs and insects that might cause harm, illness or disease. In order to protect them, a good shepherd will pour oil and "anoint" the sheep and set them apart, and because of the slick oil, the insects would no longer be a threat to the sheep.

In the same way, God commanded the priests, prophets, David and others who were called by God, to be anointed in consecration for the work God commissioned.

Part I. Anoint

Throughout the Bible and even our churches today, we see anointing used with oil to consecrate babies, pastors, missionaries and others who are called to be set apart for a specific purpose, to carry out God's plan. The actual process of anointing is not a mystic experience, it is God's people publicly agreeing with God on what he has called someone to do. Each person who has chosen to follow God, has been given a purpose to love God and to love people (Luke 10:27). God is the one who anoints, and the best anointing God gives us is the Holy Spirit, our Helper (John 14).

To add a little background, *Mashach* and *Dashen* are the Hebrew words used to describe Anointing. (Numbers 4:13; Deuteronomy 31:20; Psalm 20:3; Psalm 23:5; Proverbs 11:25, 13:4, 15:30, 28:5). Then it gets pretty exciting, *Mashach* shares the same root word used in *"Messiah"* and *"Christos,"* which is *"Christ"* in Greek (which might sound like a pretty familiar title). The Greek term for anointing is *"Chrisma"* and typically refers to the smearing of oil for a priestly or kingly task. Does that remind you of anyone who came to fulfill a very important priestly task?

The most profound prophecy in the Old Testament was about the Messiah. The word "Messiah" is translated "Anointed One;" add that with "Christ," and we recognize the titles that Jesus was given. Jesus Christ, the Messiah, the anointed one who is filled with **God's affection, purpose and love.**

In this world, the best way we can love and serve God and others is when we are filled with the love of God and the anointing of the Holy Spirit.

Remember in Chapter 3 when we were talking about the Passover and how Jesus is the Lamb of God – the perfect sacrifice. What was the price that Jesus paid to fulfil his priestly duties that God commissioned?

Jesus was able to persevere through Calvary because He was fully God and fully man and he knew God's purpose for his life on earth as the Messiah – the Anointed One. Jesus was given a big task – to take on the cup of God's wrath, let's see how Jesus responded.

> Saying, *"Father, if you are willing, remove this cup from me. Nevertheless, not my will, but yours, be done." (Luke 22:42)*

His agonized prayer at Gethsemane (Mark 14:32-42) was that of wrestling with what God had called him to do; the desperation of drinking the cup of God's wrath and fury (Jeremiah 25).

And at the ninth hour Jesus cried with a loud voice, "Eloi,
Eloi, lema sabachthani?" which means, "My God, my
God, why have you forsaken me?" (Mark 15:34)

Halleluiah! Jesus persevered in death and life because he loves us and
has a plan for us. Jesus was resolved to do the will of God the Father,
regardless of the cost and Jesus paid it in full. This was the depths of
His great love for us.

> *Be strengthened with power through his Spirit in your*
> *inner being, so that Christ may dwell in your hearts*
> *through faith—that you, being rooted and grounded in*
> *love, may have strength to comprehend with all the saints*
> *what is the breadth and length and height and depth, and*
> *to know the love of Christ that surpasses knowledge, that*
> *you may be filled with all the fullness of God. (Ephesians*
> *3:16b-18)*

A blessing is proclaiming God's favor and goodness upon someone.
God commissioned Moses and Aaron to relay a special blessing to the
Israelites:

> *The Lord bless you and keep you: The Lord make his face*
> *to shine upon you and be gracious to you; the Lord lift up*
> *his countenance upon you and give you peace."*
> *"So shall they put my name upon the people of Israel, and*
> *I will bless them." (Numbers 6:24-27)*

When Jesus' affection touches deep within our soul, healing takes place.
We experience the Loving Heavenly Father.

In Proverbs, there are a few verses that use the word *"Anoint"*
interchangeably with *"Blessing."*

Proverbs

- *11:25 Whoever brings blessing will be <u>enriched</u>, and one who waters will himself be watered.*
- *13:4 The soul of the sluggard craves and gets nothing, while the soul of the diligent is <u>richly</u> supplied.*
- *15:30 The light of the eyes rejoices the heart, and good news <u>refreshes</u> the bones.*
- *28:25 A greedy man stirs up strife, but the one who trusts in the Lord will be <u>enriched</u>.*

Jesus also used *"Anoint"* to describe the relationship that we can have with the *"Holy Spirit."*

> *But the <u>anointing</u> that you received from him abides in you, and you have no need that anyone should teach you. But as his <u>anointing</u> teaches you about everything, and is true, and is no lie—just as it has taught you, abide in him. And now, little children, abide in him, so that when he appears we may have confidence and not shrink from him in shame at his coming. If you know that he is righteous, you may be sure that everyone who practices righteousness has been born of him. (1 John 2:27-29)*

The Holy Spirit, part of the Trinity, our Helper! He is our teacher, the still small voice that guides us and helps us grow into maturity. When the Holy Spirit comes upon us, His perfect love casts out fear because the Holy Spirit Himself is love. Fear can be terrifying, but put on courage, healing takes place when we accept the truth of God, despite the fear.

> *There is no fear in love, but perfect love casts out fear. For fear has to do with punishment, and whoever fears has not been perfected in love. We love because he first loved us. (1 John 4:18)*

We are not alone! We have our Heavenly Father, Jesus Christ, the Messiah, risen Lord and we are anointed with the Holy Spirit. The community and mystery of the Triune nature of God, and we have been invited into this precious relationship. *God anoints our head with oil.* We have been set apart from this world to do the work God has given us: to Love God and to Love people, using our gifts and abilities to bring Glory to God.

Part II. With Oil

*O*il is used numerous times throughout the Bible. A bit ago we mentioned *Gethsemane*; the place where Jesus prayed before the crucifixion is explained in Bakers Encyclopedia of the Bible. The word for oil press was gatt-šemen, hence the name Garden of Gethsemane. The garden would have referred to a mature olive grove and gethsemane was the immense olive press. Jesus called God "ABBA" only one time in the New Testament; this was when He cried out to God in Gethsemane.[29]

> *And going a little farther, he fell on the ground and prayed that, if it were possible, the hour might pass from him. And he said, "Abba, Father, all things are possible for you. Remove this cup from me. Yet not what I will, but what you will." (Mark 14:35-36)*

When God anoints us, he is setting us apart to be his people with a purpose. David was anointed and set apart as King over Israel and God blessed his reign. Paul was anointed by the Holy Spirit in Acts 4:8-18 and was especially commissioned to be set apart to bear the name of Christ to the Gentiles, to kings and the children of Israel.

As we are filled up with the unconditional love of God, this same love overflows into the lives of others as we love and serve. Remember from

---

[29] Elwell, W. A., & Beitzel, B. J. (1988). In Baker encyclopedia of the Bible. Grand Rapids, MI: Baker Book House.

Chapter 2, 1 Corinthians 13 details a great picture of what this love looks like:

> *Love is patient and kind; love does not envy or boast; it is not arrogant or rude. It does not insist on its own way; it is not irritable or resentful; it does not rejoice at wrongdoing, but rejoices with the truth. Love bears all things, believes all things, hopes all things, endures all things. (1 Corinthians 13:4-7)*

I still vividly remember when God blessed me with his presence in college before I came to America. He poured out His love on me just prior to a season of darkness that came upon me. As I look back, I can now see how the hands of God were preparing me for a more difficult season that would come much later in my life. I can relate to David and his passion to love God. My passion and desire for those who lost their children by abortion came much later when I could actually process and wrestle with the reality of what had transpired, but God was gracious enough to wait for me, until I was mature enough to deal with the truth.

Also, God blessed me with His love when I was going through healing. People are chasing after so many things to fill their emptiness, not realizing we can find wholeness only through the love of God. Once we taste the love of God, we know that we do not want to crave for anything else because we tasted the joy and glory of the Heavenly Father. The battle for our loyalties is daily, but we hope with anticipation, the time when we will be with God, without sin and brokenness.

Our healing journey is a process of pursuing God's love, coming back to the heart of God. It is a personal journey. God is still waiting for us to come back to Him. The moment when David experienced the anointing after the repentance of his sin, he knew what was ahead of him, and re-focused back to God's calling. Apart from Christ, there is no complete healing in human life. By coming back to rest at the feet of Jesus, we can agree with hymn, "It is Well With My Soul" penned by hymn writer

Horatio Spafford and composed by Philip Bliss. Here is a portion of the hymn that might encourage you;

> *When peace like a river, attendeth my way,*
> *When sorrows like sea billows roll;*
> *Whatever my lot, Thou hast taught me to say*
> *It is well, it is well, with my soul.*

> *Though Satan should buffet, though trials should come,*
> *Let this blest assurance control,*
> *That Christ has regarded my helpless estate,*
> *And hath shed His own blood for my soul.*[30]

We cannot manufacture anointing. Anointing is a personal affection from God and it is His decision, not our own. We cannot pretend that "it is well with my soul" when we are not well with God. When God anoints someone, God comforts and equips them from the inside out, transforming from the very core of our being, Romans 12:1-2. God gives peace and wellness of soul to those who seek him. This is a moment for us to pause and rest in His Love and see that our soul is well.

Part III. Commission

If we have chosen to put our faith and trust in Jesus as our Savior and Lord, God anoints us with the Holy Spirit and have been commissioned to Love God, Love our Neighbor and make disciples.

> *Go therefore and make disciples of all nations, baptizing*
> *them in the name of the Father and of the Son and of the*
> *Holy Spirit, (Matthew 28:19)*

We are commissioned to make disciples, training up other believers to know and trust God, to grow and mature in our faith, in the disciplines

---

[30] Morgan, R. J. (2003). Then sings my soul: 150 of the worlds greatest hymn stories. Nashville, TN: Thomas Nelson.

of prayer, studying the word of God, fellowship with other believers in an intentional community and sharing what God has done with the world while walking in obedience to God's voice.

> *"You are the light of the world. A city set on a hill cannot be hidden. Nor do people light a lamp and put it under a basket, but on a stand, and it gives light to all in the house. In the same way, let your light shine before others, so that they may see your good works and give glory to your Father who is in heaven. (Matthew 5:14-16)*

We know that we stand out from the crowd, because we chose the side of Truth—Jesus warns us ahead of time that the world is not a friendly place. But we are still called to live a life of integrity before others, so that we can shine brightly for God.

> *"Beware of false prophets, who come to you in sheep's clothing but inwardly are ravenous wolves." (Matthew 7:15)*

There are enemies all around us, who desire to tear us down, but God is greater and stronger! A refresher from Chapter 2 – when we align with God, we choose to repent and deny the desires of our flesh. We forgive those who need forgiving, oftentimes, we need to forgive ourselves. So let us allow God to clean up and heal our hearts and minds, so that we can live life rightly for God without hindrance!

> *And he said to all, "If anyone would come after me, let him deny himself and take up his cross daily and follow me. For whoever would save his life will lose it, but whoever loses his life for my sake will save it. (Luke 9:23-24)*

> *"Behold, I am sending you out as sheep in the midst of wolves, so be wise as serpents and innocent as doves." (Matthew 10:16)*

Our commission to go out into the world, boils down to two things: Love God with every fiber of your being and then Love people with the love God has given you. Just as the Love that God loves us with overflows, spilling out into the lives that God brings into our path.

> *And he answered, "You shall love the Lord your God with all your heart and with all your soul and with all your strength and with all your mind, and your neighbor as yourself." (Luke 10:27)*

> *Jesus replied, "The most important commandment is this: 'Listen, O Israel! The Lord our God is the one and only Lord. And you must love the Lord your God with all your heart, all your soul, all your mind, and all your strength.' The second is equally important: 'Love your neighbor as yourself.' No other commandment is greater than these." (Mark 12:29-31 NLT)*

So go forth Mighty Warrior, servant of the Most High God! Into this world, armored up with Ephesians 6:10-20, making disciples by loving God and loving the people whom God brings into your sphere of influence, seeing to their needs, sharing what you have and building others up, withholding no good thing! Seeking out and taking advantage of every opportunity that God sets before you!

ॐ ☙

Jehovah-M'Kaddesh, God who sanctifies

Psalm 23:5b Discussion

- What stood out to you the most about this chapter?

- What is anointing?

- What has God called you to do? What is your purpose in life?

- What does it mean that "our cup runs over?" What would this look like in your life?

- What is the ultimate reward for believers? (John 10:28-30) (1 John 2:25) (Matthew 25:21)

- How have you experienced God's blessing and favor in your life?

- As disciples of Jesus, what has God anointed you with that is a sign of your relationship with God? (John 14-15) (1 John 2:20)

Chapter 10. House of The Lord

"Surely goodness and mercy shall follow me all the days of my life, and I shall dwell in the house of the Lord forever."
Psalm 23:6

Scripture for deeper study: Luke 7:36-50, Revelation 21-22

ഔദ

The physical and spiritual realms are at war against the souls on this earth. The enemy's days are numbered, and God's Kingdom is Coming soon! That is the power of the Good News! Jesus is coming back to deal with evil once and for all because Jesus paid the ultimate price that we can be reconciled to God and thus dwell in the house of the Lord forever. We are the object of God's unfailing and generous love!

Part I. God's Goodness & Mercy

God is so Good!

The word *tov* in Hebrew means "good" in Genesis 1, "well," and "please" in Esther 1:19, 3:9, 5:4, 5:8. God's goodness was not based on David's conduct, but on God's initiation. We cannot earn the favor of God, but rather accept His favor that has already been lavishly given to us. Many of us have a difficult time receiving goodness and mercy from God. We would much prefer to pay it back through some means. However, we soon realize that we can never pay God back for all that he has given us; nor do we need to. Isn't that great!? That is the beauty of God's goodness and mercy that is so freely given!

Mercy and grace are two words that easily get confused with one another. Grace is like a gift – giving me a free gift, which I do not deserve – eternal life! Mercy on the other hand is not giving me what I do deserve; I should be punished when I do something cruel or wrong, but instead: punishment is intentionally withheld.

Example: Jesus showed God's grace and mercy by mercifully taking my punishment of death for my sins and then graciously giving me life eternal with him.

God gave me mercy in that I did not receive death and instead He gave me grace by granting me eternal life!

The word *haset* is mostly translated as "mercy" and can also be translated as "faithful love" "steadfast love" or "loving kindness".

> *The steadfast love of the Lord never ceases; his mercies never come to an end; they are new every morning; great is your faithfulness. (Lamentations 3:22–23)*

For those who have offended us in some way, God gives us the power to forgive, bless and love them (Matthew 6:14-15; Mark 11:25). We remind ourselves of the power and love of God when we look at how we can forgive those who have wronged us. Receiving God's goodness is essential to growing in our faith.

> *Every good gift and every perfect gift is from above, coming down from the Father of lights, with whom there is no variation or shadow due to change. (James 1:17)*

When we reflect on King David's life, we can see the hands of God moving throughout his life. As a young shepherd, God gave him faith to protect his sheep from lions and bears and then protect the nation of Israel from Goliath and the Philistines, giving David great victory against many enemies. Psalms reflect many of his adventures and misadventures. God's goodness and mercy pursued David all his life. Despite of everything, he also continued to pursue God. David knew that he was followed by God's goodness, mercy, blessings and knew he belongs in God's house! As we go through different seasons of life, like David, we will see the goodness and mercy of God over and over again.

The opposite of mercy is condemnation.

> *Therefore there is now no condemnation for those who are in Christ Jesus. (Romans 8:1 NASB)*

I was one of over 70 million people who are affected by abortion and at one time, I felt condemned because all I could hear was voices of judgement pointing out abortion experience as horrific through medias and from the reaction of people. I am thankful because the voice of compassion and God's rich mercy is prevailing. I choose to believe what God says and because I have placed my hope and trust in Jesus, I know there is no condemnation for me. Jesus described a beautiful parable in Luke 7:36-50 about a sinful woman who came to Jesus and was forgiven.

> *"Therefore I tell you, her sins, which are many, are forgiven—for she loved much. But he who is forgiven little, loves little." And he said to the woman, "Your faith has saved you; go in peace." (Luke 7:47, 50)*

May we walk in mercy and grace without condemnation so that we can serve God wholeheartedly and without hindrance.

> *Therefore, since we are surrounded by so great a cloud of witnesses, let us also lay aside every weight, and sin which clings so closely, and let us run with endurance the race that is set before us, looking to Jesus, the founder and perfecter of our faith, who for the joy that was set before him endured the cross, despising the shame, and is seated at the right hand of the throne of God. (Hebrews 12:1-2)*

Now that we understand a little about God's goodness and mercy, what does it mean that *goodness and mercy shall follow* me? The word "follow" in this verse is a very intense form of the word, follow as in unrelenting in its pursuit, even to run after something. So God's goodness and mercy run after and actively pursue us, all of our days.

God's goodness and mercy were given a time frame: ALL THE DAYS OF MY LIFE. God's goodness and mercy are blessings that are not based on our conduct or life circumstances, but based on who He is, unchanging, promise keeper.

> *Forever, O Lord, your word is firmly fixed in the heavens. (Psalm 119:89)*

In the midst of difficult times, we remember God's goodness and mercy: Psalm 68:4-10 expresses our worship of our wonderful God:

> *Sing to God, sing praises to his name; lift up a song to him who rides through the deserts; his name is the Lord; exult before him!*
> *Father of the fatherless and protector of widows is God in his holy habitation.*
> *God settles the solitary in a home; he leads out the prisoners to prosperity, but the rebellious dwell in a parched land*
> *O God, when you went out before your people when you marched through the wilderness, Selah*
> *the earth quaked, the heavens poured down rain, before God, the One of Sinai, before God, the God of Israel.*
> *Rain in abundance, O God, you shed abroad; you restored your inheritance as it languished; your flock found a dwelling in it; in your goodness, O God, you provided for the needy.*

We serve a Big God who is worthy of all praise!

Praise him, sun and moon, praise him, all you shining stars! Praise him, you highest heavens, and you waters above the heavens! Let them praise the name of the Lord! For he commanded and they were created. And he established them forever and ever; he gave a decree, and it shall not pass away. (Psalm 145:3-6)

God is patient and he does not change. His promises are true forever. May the Lord be good and merciful to you today.

The Lord is gracious and merciful, slow to anger and abounding in steadfast love. The Lord is good to all, and his mercy is over all that he has made. (Psalm 145:8-9)

Part II. Dwell

For the Israelites, the word, "dwell," has a special meaning. They were nomads or wanderers who built their homes wherever their flocks took them. Having a home is very meaningful. But at the same time, their lifestyle reflects our spiritual state, we are on earth for a short time as sojourners, but our house is in heaven with God.

To Dwell means the house of the Lord becomes our permanent resident. Strong number 3427. יָשַׁב yashab (442a), a prim. root; to sit, remain, dwell, is the Hebrew word dwell.

The word for God's dwelling is "Shekinah."

Shekinah: Transliteration of a Hebrew word meaning "the one who dwells" or "that which dwells." ...God, whose dwelling is in heaven, also dwells on earth. In its narrower uses the term is applied to the "shekinah glory," the visible pillar of fire and smoke that dwelled in the midst of Israel at Sinai (Ex 19:16–18), in the wilderness (40:34–38), and in the temple (1 Kgs 6:13; 8:10–13; 2 Chr 6:1, 2). He now dwells in the hearts of his people (Eph. 3:17–19). The Holy Spirit dwells in believers (1 Cor. 3:16; 2

Tim. 1:14). We are exhorted to "let the word of God dwell in us richly" (Col. 3:16; Ps. 119:11).[31]

What do you think of when you think of home? I think of a place where my mom and dad were because of the sweet memories. My brothers and sister and I would play outside until sunset and then hear the sounds of dinner being prepared by several moms from the neighborhood and then the smell of delicious food being prepared was the cue to head home. These cozy feelings make me feel warm inside. I loved to be at my grandmother's house because I knew I was loved and accepted. Even if we were not eating a fancy dinner at my grandmother's, the food was so delicious.

A healthy home is a place where we feel safe and loved.

In the Old Testament, God's dwelling place with mankind was limited in the time of Moses to the pillars of fire, clouds and then the veil in the temple where the ark of the covenant was. After Jesus' death and resurrection, the veil of the temple was torn and God's dwelling place changed.

> *And I heard a loud voice from the throne saying, "Behold, the dwelling place of God is with man. He will dwell with them, and they will be his people, and God himself will be with them as their God. (Revelation 21:3)*

God desires to find his home in you. Philippians 1:6 – God will continue His work in you until He returns! That means that God isn't finished with his plans for you! If you are not already a part of a community of believers, ask God to find one and seek out people who love God. Be the one to show lavish, extraordinary love to others, seek God in everything. Until God calls us to our heavenly home, we find our temporary residence here on earth, with God dwelling within us. There is no perfect church or community of believers, but here on earth is where we get to

---

[31] Elwell, W. A., & Beitzel, B. J. (1988). In Baker encyclopedia of the Bible. Grand Rapids, MI: Baker Book House.

practice. We share the grace with others and experience the grace from others. We get to practice loving and working together, seeing to each other's needs, mourning with those who mourn and rejoicing with those who rejoice (Romans 12:15). By sharing our burdens, the hardships get divided, and by sharing good news, our joys get multiplied!

> *Finally, brothers, rejoice. Aim for restoration, comfort one another, agree with one another, live in peace; and the God of love and peace will be with you. (2 Corinthians 13:11)*

I think the church is designed to be a glimpse of the house of the Lord to come. It does not have to be fancy, (Heaven of course, has streets of gold—Revelation 21:21) but homey, where the presence of God dwells, where weary people can come, rest and be healed. We yearn for dwelling in the house of the Lord, our refuge.

> *And I saw no temple in the city, for its temple is the Lord God the Almighty and the Lamb. And the city has no need of sun or moon to shine on it, for the glory of God gives it light, and its lamp is the Lamb. (Revelation 21:22-23)*

Part III. Citizen of Heaven

We all are going to go home, our permanent home where there is no sorrow, pain, evil or sickness. This home is described in Revelation 20-22.

> *He will wipe away every tear from their eyes, and death shall be no more, neither shall there be mourning, nor crying, nor pain anymore, for the former things have passed away." (Revelation 21:4)*

Are you looking for this home? This is where we belong! The world does not know us, because we are not of this world, but our citizenship has been transferred from earth to heaven!

But we are citizens of heaven, where the Lord Jesus Christ lives. And we are eagerly waiting for him to return as our Savior. He will take our weak mortal bodies and change them into glorious bodies like his own, using the same power with which he will bring everything under his control. (Philippians 3:20-21 NLT)

Psalm 27:4 describes how David loves the house of the Lord. One thing he will ask of God is to dwell in the house of God all the days of his life.

> *The Lord is my light and my salvation; whom shall I fear? The Lord is the stronghold of my life; of whom shall I be afraid?*
>
> *When evildoers assail me to eat up my flesh, my adversaries and foes, it is they who stumble and fall.*
>
> *Though an army encamp against me, my heart shall not fear; though war arise against me, yet I will be confident.*
>
> ***One thing have I asked of the Lord, that will I seek after: that I may dwell in the house of the Lord all the days of my life,*** *to gaze upon the beauty of the Lord and to inquire in his temple.*
>
> *For he will hide me in his shelter in the day of trouble; he will conceal me under the cover of his tent; he will lift me high upon a rock. (Psalm 27:1-5)*

Until we are called to our permanent home heavenward, where our Heavenly Father is, we are commissioned to fulfill God's call on our lives while on earth. We get to worship God freely and experience His goodness and mercy as He continually transforms us, body, heart, mind and soul. We are to love. May God grant us His goodness and mercy while we share Psalm 23 with others who desperately need His abounding and unfailing love.

Part IV: Forever "No less days to sing His praise"

*E*ternity has already begun! We can know God's peace and rest in the knowledge that our time with God has already started and no one is going to end it – this is our hope and confidence.

> *And this is **eternal life**, that they know you, the only true God, and Jesus Christ whom you have sent. (John 17:3)*

> *I give them **eternal life**, and they will never perish, and no one will snatch them out of my hand. (John 10:28)*

Isn't that great!? There's no competition, God's got ahold of us and has given us eternal life. I want to finish with the lyrics of a hymn you might be familiar with.

Amazing Grace by John Newton
Amazing grace! how sweet the sound,
That saved a wretch; like me!
I once was lost, but now am found,
Was blind, but now I see.
'Twas grace that taught my heart to fear,
And grace my fears relieved;
How precious did that grace appear
The hour I first believed!

The Lord hath promised good to me,
His word my hope secures;
He will my shield and portion be
As long as life endures.

When we've been there ten thousand years,
Bright shining as the sun,
We've no less days to sing God's praise
Than when we first begun.

We were once lost in darkness, and maybe you still are, but God never lost us; he is the Good Shepherd. He knows exactly where we are, and he is calling for you; are you responding to his still, quiet voice? Even when we walk through a dark valley where death seems to be looming, God is there, he desires to protect and guide us from the numerous enemies that threaten us, with His rod and staff. Even in the midst of our enemies, we can be at peace and receive nourishment at the Lord's table because He has anointed us with his love, empowered us with the Holy Spirit and commissioned us to share this love to the world. We have a confidence and hope because we are now united with Christ forevermore! God will prepare a table before us in the presence of the enemies; we will dwell in His presence forever and ever.

> *All praise to God, the Father of our Lord Jesus Christ,*
> *who has blessed us with every spiritual blessing in the*
> *heavenly realms because we are united with Christ.*
> *(Ephesians 1:3 NLT)*

ഌ രു

El-Shaddai, God Almighty

Psalm 23:6 Discussion

- What stood out the most to you about this chapter?

- What does it mean that goodness and mercy shall follow me all the days of my life? How have you experienced God at work in these areas?

- What does "follow" mean?

- What do you imagine the house of the Lord to look like?

- How can your home resemble the house of the Lord?

- Do you have a community of people or a local church that you can be connected with? (Hebrews 10:24-25)

- Take a moment to reflect on the time that we have spent diving into Psalm 23.

- What has God been showing you about himself?

- What has God been challenging you with through Psalm 23?

৪০০৪

O' Precious child of the King of kings, peace to you, persevere in the midst of difficulties and thrive in your relationships as you trust God. Walk by faith as the author and finisher of our faith, who, for the joy of you, He endured the cross and is now seated at the right hand of God in heaven, and He is coming back for us, so very soon! (2 Corinthians 5:7; James 1; Hebrews 12:1-2).

How Wondrous! How Marvelous! We get to be in fellowship with our Heavenly Father from now until forevermore and that means we have no less days to Sing God's Praise!

I Love you! Go in His Peace!
Shalom

৪০০৪

About the Author
Inseong Kim

Hello, I am Inseong Kim, artist, author, executive producer, Host of In His Love at New Faith Talk 1360AM KPXQ+.

"Our heart is to share the hope and encouragement to those who are hurting as well as hear everyone's heart from the various angles."

Inseong is the wife of Steven and a mother of three children. God allowed her to remain faithful to serve her family as the most important ministry. It has not been an easy journey in this culture. Inseong is post-abortive, but saved by the grace of God. The love of God was poured out on her and her family through the love and ministry of a beautiful church, Calvary Community Church, in Phoenix. Inseong's special mission is to address the combination of abortion and legalism that can cause so much damage in us, our families, our church and our nation. The desire of Inseong's heart is to share the love of Jesus with those who experienced an abortion, or any trauma caused by abuse. When truth abounds, and grace is shared properly, the fruit of freedom can be found. We are reminded of the more than fifty million babies who are dead, yet we have forgotten the millions of mothers and fathers who are wounded and broken. It is time for us to open our arms to those who are hurting and minister them. Please tune in our program, In His Love, on Sunday 7:00 a.m.

She attended a prominent woman's university, Ewha University in South Korea and studied Special Education. Also, she earned BS degree in Actuarial Science at Ohio State University. She is a student at Phoenix Seminary.

Most of her life, she has supported her husband, Steven, his education and business as a dentist to be one of the top dentists in Phoenix, Arizona. She enjoys her extra time as an artist, a radio host, and author. She was the Executive producer of a documentary film, My Dear Sammy.

www.inseongkim.org

Home   About   Gallery ⌄   Store   Event   Contact

HOPE IN MISSION, LLC

Home   Author   Shop Online

4 GB USB with messages

inhislove.tv

Home   Be There   About   Special Note   Archives   Resources

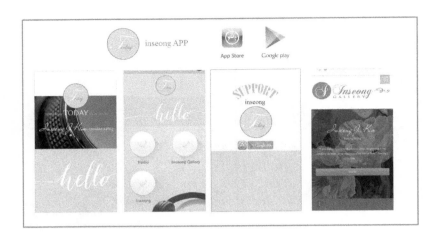

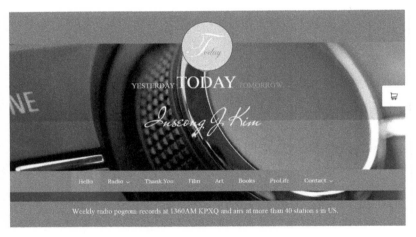

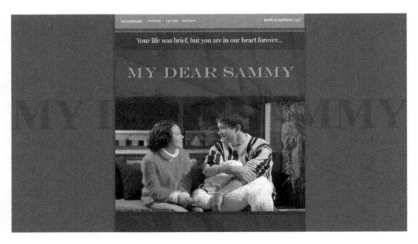

About the Author
Elizabeth Fair

Greetings! I am Elizabeth Fair, a daughter of the King of Kings, a citizen of Heaven and presently reside in the beautiful desert of Phoenix, Arizona.

Elizabeth finds great joy in serving God. Currently she works in the field of Information Technology, attended Arizona State University, and then Grand Canyon University where she completed a Bachelor's in Health Care Administration, Master's in Business Administration and presently pursuing a PhD. She has pursued many opportunities to love and serve others. She has spent many years facilitating Bible studies, camp programming, writing curriculum, serving on boards and committees, investing in mentoring and organizing events for youth and young adults. She is passionate about seeing God mature His people through fulfilling the Great Commission of discipleship; by loving God and loving people.

Complementary Resources

Chapter 1. The Lord is My Shepherd

A Shepherd Looks at Psalm 23
Keller, W. P. (2007). *A shepherd looks at Psalm 23*. Grand Rapids, MI: Zondervan. ISBN-13: 978-0310274414

Lead Like Jesus
Blanchard, K. & Hodges, P. (2005). Lead like Jesus: lessons from the greatest leadership role model of all times. Nashville, TN: Thomas Nelson. ISBN-13: 978-1400314201

Chapter 2. I shall not want

Case for Christ
Strobel, L. (2016). *Case for Christ*. Grand Rapids, MI: Zondervan. ISBN-13: 978-0310345862

Lord I want to Know You
Arthur, K. (1992). *Lord, I want to know you: a devotional study of the names of God*. New York, NY: Waterbrook Press. ISBN-13: 978-1578564392

Chapter 3. Green Pastures

Boundaries
Cloud, H., & Townsend, J. S. (2012). *Boundaries: When to say yes, when to say no to take control of your life.* Grand Rapids, MI: Zondervan. ISBN-13: 978-0310247456

Secrets of the Vine
Wilkinson, B. (2001). *Secrets of the Vine: Breaking through to abundance.* Sisters, OR: Multnomah Publishers Inc.
ISBN-13: 978-1590524961

Chapter 4. Restoration by Still Water

Moving Mountains
Eldredge, J. (2017). *Moving Mountains Praying with Passion, Confidence, and Authority.* Nashville, TN: Thomas Nelson. ISBN-13: 978-0718088590

TrueFaced
Thrall, B., McNicol, B., & Lynch, J. (2004). *Truefaced: Trust God and others with who you really are.* Colorado Springs, CO: NavPress. ISBN-13: 978-1576836934

Chapter 5. Paths of Righteousness

Case for a Creator
Strobel, L. (2004). *The Case for a Creator.* Grand Rapids, MI: Zondervan. ISBN-13: 978-0310242093

Sacred Marriage
Thomas, G. (2015). *Sacred marriage: What if God designed marriage to make us holy more than to make us happy?* Grand Rapids, MI: Zondervan. ISBN-13: 978-0310337379

Chapter 6. You are with me

Life Together
Bonhoeffer, D. (1954). *Life Together: the classic exploration of Christian community.* New York, NY: HarperCollins Publishers. ISBN-13: 978-0060608521

Love Does
Goff, B. (2012). *Love does - discover a secretly incredible life in an ordinary world.* Nashville, TN: Thomas Nelson. ISBN-13: 978-1400203758

Chapter 7. Rod & Staff Comfort me

Names of God devotional
Hudson, C. D. (2016). *100 names of God: Daily devotional.* Carson, CA: Rose Publishing. ISBN-13: 978-1628622911

That the World May Know: Faith Lessons by Ray Vander Laan https://www.thattheworldmayknow.com/

Chapter 8. More than a Conqueror

Case for Faith
Strobel, L. (2014). *The case for faith: A journalist investigates the toughest objections to Christianity.* Grand Rapids, MI: Zondervan. ISBN-13: 978-0310339298

On Being a Servant of God
Wiersby, W. (1993). *On Being a Servant of God.* Grand Rapids, MI: Baker Books. ISBN-13: 978-0801068195

Chapter 9. Anoint & Blessing

DNA of Relationships
Smalley, G. (2007). *The DNA of relationships.* Wheaton, IL: Tyndale House. ISBN-13: 978-0842355322

The 5 Love Languages
Chapman, G. (2015). *The 5 Love Languages.* Chicago, IL: Northfield Publishing. ISBN-13: 978-0802412706

Chapter 10. House of The Lord

Emotional Intelligence 2.0
Bradberry, T., Greaves, J., & Lencioni, P. (2009). *Emotional intelligence 2.0.* San Diego, CA: TalentSmart. ISBN-13: 978-0974320625

Imagine Heaven
Burke, J. (2015). *Imagine heaven: Near-death experiences, Gods promises, and the exhilarating future that awaits you.* Grand Rapids, MI: Baker Books. ISBN-13: 978-0801015267

My Heart – Christ's Home
Munger, R. B. (1986). *My heart-- Christs home.* Downers Grove, IL: Inter-Varsity Press. ISBN-13: 978-0877840756

Discipleship Resources

The Wheel[a], by the Navigators

A simple illustration that dives into practical ways to grow in your relationship with God: *Christ* is the center, talk with God through *Prayer*, get to know God by studying the *Bible*, *Fellowship* with other Christians and *Evangelism*, sharing God's work in your life. The whole wheel moves forward through *obedience*.

The Navigators also have additional resources on prayer, studying the Bible, promises and assurances as Christians and our identity in Christ.

Since we presently live in the **digital age**, a few electronic resources that might be helpful:

- Bible App: Bible App & Web
- Blueletterbible: study Bible detailed, App & Web
- Derek Prince Ministries: App/Radio/Youtube/Web
- DesiringGod.com: Sermons by topic, App & Web
- Echo App: Prayer reminder
- First15: Daily Devotional – Twitter, App & Web
- Focus on the Family: Family/Relationship Resources
- OnePlace: Radio Sermons – App & Web
- Pluggedinonline: Movie/Music Review, App & Web
- RightNowMedia: Bible Studies, App & Web
- The Bible Project: Video, Blog & Youtube
- Verses: App to help memorize scripture

References

Allender, D. B. (2005). *How children raise parents: The art of listening to your family.* Colorado Springs, CO: Waterbrook Press.

Anderson, N. T. (2000). *The bondage breaker.* Eugene, Or.: Harvest House.

Balswick, J. K., & Balswick, J. O. (2008). *Authentic human sexuality: An integrated Christian approach.* Downers Grove, IL: IVP Academic.

Bauer, D. R., & Traina, R. A. (2011). *Inductive Bible study: A comprehensive guide to the practice of hermeneutics.* Grand Rapids, Michigan: Baker Academic.

Beckman, L. J., & Harvey, S. M. (1999). *The new civil war: The psychology, culture, and politics of abortion.* Washington, D.C.: American Psychological Association.

Bell, M. C. (1985). *Calvin and Scottish theology: The doctrine of assurance.* Edinburgh: Handsel Press.

Benner, J. A. (2004). *The ancient Hebrew language and alphabet: Understanding the ancient Hebrew language of the Bible based on ancient Hebrew culture and thought.* College Station, TX: Virtualbookworm. com Pub.

Benner, J. A. (2005). *The ancient Hebrew lexicon of the Bible: Hebrew letters, words and roots defined within their ancient cultural context.* College Station, TX: Virtualbookworm.com Publishing.

Benner, J. A. (2009). *Ancient Hebrew dictionary: 1000 verbs and nouns of the Hebrew Bible.* College Station, TX: Virtualbookworm.com Pub.

Bottke, A. (2008). *Setting boundaries with your adult children.* Eugene, Or.: Harvest House.

Brown, C. (1975). *The New international dictionary of New Testament theology.* Grand Rapids, MI: Zondervan.

Bruner, R. F., & Carr, S. D. (2009). *The Panic of 1907: Lessons learned from the markets perfect storm.* Hoboken, NJ: John Wiley & Sons.

Bullinger, E. W. (2012). *Figures of speech used in the Bible.* New York: Cosimo Classics.

Bunyan, J. (n.d.). *The Pilgrims progress.* Chicago: Moody Press.

Burtchaell, J. T. (1980). *Abortion parley: Papers delivered at the National Conference on Abortion held at the University of Notre Dame in October 1979.* Kansas City: Andrews and McMeel.

Carlson, D. L. (2015). *Overcoming hurts & anger.* Eugene: Harvest House.

Charles darwins the life od erasmus darwin. (2011). Cambridge: Cambridge Univ Press.

Chesler, E. (2007). *Woman of valor: Margaret Sanger and the birth control movement in America.* New York: Simon & Schuster Paperbacks.

Chilton, D. (1990). *Productive Christians in an age of guilt-manipulations: A biblical response to Ronald J. Sider.* Tyler, Taxas: Institute for Christ Economics.

Cloud, H., & Townsend, J. (1992). *Boundaries: When To Say Yes, When To Say No To Take Control Of Yo.* Grand Rapids: Zondervan.

Cloud, H. (2016). *The Power of the Other: The Startling Effect Other People Have on You.* New York: HarperBusiness.

Davis, D. R. (2007). *2 Samuel: Out of every adversity.* Fearn, Ross-Shire: Christian Focus.

Delhousaye, D., & Brewer, B. (2008). *The personal journal of Solomon: The secrets of Kohelet ; a commentary of Ecclesiastes for the common reader.* Longwood, FL: Xulon Press.

Dever, M. E. (2011). *Proclaiming a cross-centered theology.* Wheaton, Ill: Crossway Books.

Devlin, K. J. (2002). *The language of mathematics: Making the invisible visible.* New York: W.H. Freeman.

Dickerson, J. S. (2013). *The great evangelical recession: 6 factors that will crash the American church-- and how to prepare*. Grand Rapids, MI: Baker Books.

Driscoll, M., & Breshears, G. (2008). *Death by love: Letters from the cross*. Wheaton, IL: Crossway Books.

Farbridge, M. H. (2007). *Studies in biblical and semitic symbolism*. Place of publication not identified: Wipf & Stock.

Forward, S., & Buck, C. (2002). *Toxic parents: Overcoming their hurtful legacy and reclaiming your life*. New York: Bantam Books.

Forward, S., & Frazier, D. (2002). *Toxic in-laws: Loving strategies for protecting your marriage*. New York, NY: Quill.

Fowler, P. B. (1987). *Abortion: Toward an evangelical consensus*. Portland, Or.: Multnomah Press.

Frame, J. M. (2008). *The doctrine of the Christian life*. Phillipsburg, NJ: P & R Publishing.

Geisler, N. L. (2007). *Christian Apologetics*. Grand Rapids: Baker Book House.

Georges, J., & Baker, M. D. (2016). *Ministering in honor-shame cultures: Biblical foundations and practical essentials*. Downers Grove, IL: IVP Academic.

Georges, J., & Baker, M. D. (2016). *Ministering in honor-shame cultures: Biblical foundations and practical essentials*. Downers Grove, IL: IVP Academic.

Glendon, M. A. (1987). *Abortion and divorce in western law*. Cambridge: Harvard University Press.

Gorney, C. (1998). *Articles of faith: A frontline history of the abortion wars*. New York, NY: Simon & Schuster.

Grant, R. G. (2005). *Battle: A visual journey through 5,000 years of combat*. New York, NY: Dorling Kindersley.

Gray, M. H. (2015). *Tour To The Sepulchres Of Etruria, In 1839 (Classic Reprint)*. S.L.: Forgotten Books.

Grudem, W. A. (2000). *Systematic theology: An introduction to biblical doctrine*. Grand Rapids, MI: Zondervan Pub. House.

Grudem, W. A. (2010). *Politics according to the Bible: A comprehensive resource for understanding modern political issues in light of scripture*. Grand Rapids, MI: Zondervan.

Grun, B., & Stein, W. (1982). *The Timetables of history: A horizontal linkage of people and events*. New York: Simon & Schuster.

Hamilton-Gray, (1843). *The history of Etruria: Tarchun and his times: From the foundation of Tarquinia to the foundations of Rome*. London: Hatchard and Son.

Hanegraaff, H. (1993). *Christianity in crisis*. Eugene, Or.: Harvest House.

Harris, R. L., Archer, G. L., & Waltke, B. K. (1981). *Theological Wordbook of the Old Testament*. Chicago: Moody press.

Hill, A. E., & Walton, J. H. (2009). *A survey of the Old Testament*. Grand Rapids, MI: ZondervanPublishing House.

Hunt, J. M. (2017). *Demolishing strongholds*. Eugene, OR: Harvest House.

Hunter, W. B. (1986). *The God who hears*. Downers Grove, IL: InterVarsity Press.

James, C. C. (2001). *When life and beliefs collide: How knowing God makes a difference*. Grand Rapids, MI: Zondervan.

Johnston, G. F. (2003). *Abortion from the religious and moral perspective: An annotated bibliography*. Westport, CT: Praeger Pub.

Johnston, S. I. (2004). *Religions of the ancient world: A guide*. Cambridge: The Belknap Press of Harvard University Press.

Josephus, F., Whiston, W., & Maier, P. L. (1999). *The new complete works of Josephus*. Grand Rapids, MI: Kregel.

Ketterman, G. H., & Hazard, D. (2000). *When you cant say "I forgive you": Breaking the bonds of anger and hurt*. Colorado Springs, CO: NavPress.

Kim, I. J. (2010). *Rest in His love, our Redeemer, Jesus Christ*. Xulon Press.

KIM, I. J. (2012). *Calling Beyond Healing*. Xulon Press.

Klein, M. (2003). *Rainbows end: The crash of 1929*. Oxford: Oxford University Press.

Klein, W. W., Blomberg, C., & Hubbard, R. L. (2004). *Introduction to biblical interpretation*. Nashville, TN: Thomas Nelson.

Laurie, G. (2015). *Do you want to change your life?*United States: Allen David Books.

Luhan, M. D. (1985). *Movers and shakers*. Albuquerque: University of New Mexico Press.

Lundgaard, K. (1998). *The enemy within: Straight talk about the power and defeat of sin*. Phillipsburg, NJ: P & R.

MacArthur, J. (2005). *The MacArthur Bible commentary*. Nashville: Nelson Reference & Electronic.

Macleod, D. (1998). *The person of Christ*. Downers Grove, IL: InterVarsity Press.

McBride, K. (2013). *Will I ever be good enough?: Healing the daughters of narcissistic mothers*. New York: Atria Paperback.

Merrill, Eugene H. (2008) *Kingdom of priests: a history of Old Testament Israel*. Grand Rapids, MI, Baker Academic.

Metaxas, E. (2017). *Martin Luther: The Man Who Rediscovered God and Changed the World*. Penguin Publishing Group.

Moreland, J. P. (2017). *Theistic evolution: A scientific, philosophical, and theological critique*. Wheaton, IL: Crossway.

Morgan, R. J. (2008). *The promise: How God works all things together for good*. Nashville, TN: B & H Pub. Group.

Moscati, S., & Moscati, S. (1973). *The world of the Phoenicians*. London: Cardinal.

Nelsons New illustrated Bible dictionary. (1995). Nashville, TN: Thomas Nelson.

Newsinger, J. (1999). *Shaking the world: John Reeds revolutionary journalism*. London: Bookmarks.

OBrien, C. (2009). *The Fall Of Empires*. New York: Fall River Press.

Olasky, M. N. (1992). *Abortion rites: A social history of abortion in America*. Wheaton, IL: Crossways Books.

Packer, J. I., & Nystrom, C. (2005). *Never beyond hope: How God touches & uses imperfect people*. Downers Grove, IL: InterVarsity Press.

Palmer, L. J., Palmer, X. Z., & Palmer, L. J. (2009). *Encyclopedia of abortion in the United States*. Jefferson, NC: McFarland &.

Peel, W. C. (2009). *What God does when men lead: The power and potential of regular guys*. Carol Stream, IL: Tyndale House.

Peterson, E. H. (1996). *Five smooth stones for pastoral work*. Grand Rapids, Mich: W.B. Eerdmans.

Peterson, E. H. (2012). *The pastor: A memoir*. New York: HarperOne.

Piper, J. (2008). *Spectacular sins: And their global purpose in the glory of Christ*. Wheaton, IL: Crossway Books.

Prince, D. (1976). *How to fast successfully*. Springdale, PA: Whitaker House.

Rae, S. B. (2009). *Moral choices: An introduction to ethics*. Grand Rapids, MI: Zondervan.

Rebanks, J. (2016). *The shepherds view: Modern photographs from an ancient landscape*. New York: Flatiron Books.

Roth, A. G. (2012). *Katva ḳadisha = Aramaic English New Testament: Mari: A compilation, annotation and translation of the eastern original Aramaic New Testament Peshitta text.* Bellingham, WA: Netzari Press.

Rubin, E. R. (1999). *The abortion controversy: A documentary history.* Westport: Greenwood Press.

Rudnick, L. P. (2000). *Mabel Dodge Luhan: New woman, new worlds.* Albuquerque: University of New Mexico Press.

Schaeffer, F. A. (2005). *How should we then live?: The rise and decline of western thought and culture.* Place of publication not identified: Crossway Books.

Schlesinger, H. I. (1937). *General Chemistry*(Third ed.). Longmans, Green, and.

Segers, M. C., & Byrnes, T. A. (1995). *Abortion politics in American states.* Armonk, NY: M.E. Sharpe.

Solomon, R. (2008). *The little book of mathematical principles, theories, & things.* New York: Metro Books.

Stanley, C. F. (1992). *The wonderful Spirit-filled life.* Nashville: Thomas Nelson.

Stanley, C. F. (1995). *How to listen to God.* Nashville, TN: Thomas Nelson Pub.

Stilman, A. (2010). *Grammatically correct: The essential guide to spelling, style, usage, grammar, and punctuation.* Cincinnati, OH: Writers Digest Books.

Strong, J. (1995). *New Strongs exhaustive concordance of the Bible: With main concordance, appendix to the main concordance, Hebrew and Aramaic dictionary of the Old Testament, Greek dictionary of the New Testament.* Nashville, TN: Thomas Nelson.

Swindoll, C. R. (1997). *Esther: A woman of strength & dignity: Profiles in character.* Nashville, TN: Word Publishing.

L. (1982). *The practice of the presence of God.* Springdale, PA.: Whitaker House.

Thomas, G. (2009). *Pure pleasure: Why do Christians feel so bad about feeling good?*Grand Rapids, MI: Zondervan.

Tracy, S. R. (2008). *Mending the soul: Understanding and healing abuse.* Grand Rapids, MI: Zondervan.

Uglow, J. S. (2002). *The lunar men: Five friends whose curiosity changed the world.* New York: Farrar, Straus, and Giroux.

Vought, J. (1991). *Post-abortion trauma: 9 steps to recovery.* Grand Rapids, MI: Zondervan Pub. House.

Wilson, S. D. (2002). *Released from shame: Moving beyond the pain of the past.* Downers Grove, IL: InterVarsity Press.

CPSIA information can be obtained
at www.ICGtesting.com
Printed in the USA
BVHW080843030419
544470BV00004B/656/P

9 781973 657750